ples of
Micro
Economics

Neil Fuller BSc (Econ), MSc, MCIPS

Revisions by
Nigel Proctor BA, MA (Econ), PGCE

003

TUDOR

Published in Great Britain by Tudor Business Publishing Ltd.

First published 1987
Reprinted with revisions 1990, 1993

Second edition 1997

British Library Cataloguing in Publication Data:
A catalogue record for this book is available from the British Library

ISBN   1–872807–57–7

Cover design by T/S Graphics

Typeset in 10/12 pt Palatino by GreenGate Publishing Services,Tonbridge, Kent
Printed in Great Britain by the Athenaeum Press, Gateshead, Tyne & Wear

Contents

Introduction

The new edition of this book has been completely revised, not only in its content but also its layout and design. All the data, background information and text has been up-dated to meet the needs of today's readers.

As with the earlier editions, the book is intended to assist students who have little, or no, prior knowledge of micro economics to rapidly grasp the main principles of the subject. It covers the requirements of most courses including A-level, the first year of degree courses, the foundation stages of the professional bodies, graduate conversion courses, and should be particularly suitable for those on single semesters in micro economics. It has proved especially suitable for those students with no knowledge of the subject who need to progress rapidly to a high level of understanding.

Experience has shown that students frequently have difficulty at the outset where the issues are clouded by an excess of data and empirical results, however essential this may be at a later stage. The objective here is therefore to produce a concise text which explains in a straightforward manner the principles of micro economics. It is essential however that students themselves keep abreast of events by reading more widely in the press and relevant journals, in particular in such areas as competition law, mergers and acquisitions, and general trends in industry.

It is suggested that students read a chapter of the book and then test their understanding of the material they have studied by attempting the self-assessment questions at the end of the chapter. These questions can all be answered from the material within the chapter.

Where mathematical proofs are involved they have been put into appendices in order to avoid confusing the less mathematically able student; it is important however that all students read through the appendices and attempt to follow the reasoning within them. Since the publication of the first edition of this book concern with the environment has grown into a major controversy and the chapter on environmental economics helps to clarify the issues and set them in a theoretical framework in order that a sound analysis of the problems involved can be made.

Another area where it has been necessary to question some of the issues discussed in the earlier edition is that of diseconomies of scale. Although it is not possible to draw any firm conclusions, at least some organisations seem to be challenging the inevitability of diseconomies of scale, and at least may be successfully delaying them by the introduction of new management techniques and the use of information technology to improve control. I am grateful for the help given to me by Nigel Proctor both in restructuring the material and for his assistance in up-dating the contents. I would also like to acknowledge Richard Ledward of Staffordshire University for his advice and assistance with the data collection, and my colleague David Barnes for his assistance and comments.

Neil Fuller 1997

1

Basic concepts

1 Economics

Economics is the study of how the human race can provide for its material well-being. As such it analyses the ways in which people can apply their skills, efforts and knowledge to the available natural resources in order to produce those goods and services which will satisfy their wants.

2 Social science

proved confirmed

Economics is a social science. Social because it studies mankind and society, although unlike other social sciences it studies only one aspect of mankind's behaviour; and science because of the method of study. Economics attempts wherever possible to adopt a scientific approach. Therefore it attempts to use only positive statements which are those which can be verified by appeal to the facts, rather than normative statements, which are frequently matters of opinion, or **value judgements**, about which we may all hold different but equally valid opinions. Value judgements are more a matter for policy makers to decide in line with their perception of society's preferences, whilst economists are more concerned with finding the most efficient, or lowest cost, method of achieving a given objective. It cannot be ignored however that inevitably economic decisions will be influenced indirectly by social and political considerations.

Unlike other scientists, however, the economist cannot experiment as it is not possible to have a controlled experiment. In order to compensate for the lack of control over other variables economists frequently include the expression ceteris paribus (cet. par.), meaning 'other things being equal', when they make a statement, which means that they believe the statement to be true provided other factors remain unchanged.

3 Opportunity cost

As resources are always limited in supply and human wants appear to be insatiable then we always require more goods than are available. As resources are limited and wants are insatiable mankind is continually forced to make choices. It is the making of these choices which is central to the study of economics. Every time we make a decision to produce something we choose to forego the alternative which we could have produced, the cost of this foregone alternative is known as the **opportunity cost**. Opportunity cost also applies every time we make a decision to buy something as consumers, and every time we make a collective decision as a nation; for example if we produce Concorde those resources will not be available to build roads or hospitals.

4 Scarcity and choice

Scarcity therefore forces us to make **choices**, and as we make choices we are forced to **sacrifice** other things, in other words we are forced to economise. Normally however the choice is not between one good or another, but how many more of one good should we have and how much less of another. Scarcity and choice are therefore central to the study of economics. Those goods which are produced from our scarce resources are referred to as **economic goods**, and as they are scarce they have a **price**; the price being relative to their scarcity. Goods or resources which are not scarce but are available in unlimited quantities do not have a price, e.g. air; there is no need therefore to economise with them, and so they do not enter the study of economics.

5 Wants

Wants can be satisfied by the production of either tangible goods or the enjoyment of services. In the study of economics anything which satisfies a want is said to have **utility**. Different goods however produce different amounts of utility, or the same good can produce different amounts of utility in different places or at different times, for example water has a different utility in a dry country than in Britain.

6 Goods and services

As goods are produced they are then consumed and the act of consumption provides the required utility, but in so doing creates a new want. There is therefore an endless round of production, consumption, and the creation of new wants leading to new production. The rate at which goods are consumed however differs.

Consumer goods are consumed over a relatively short time period and we receive utility directly from their use, for example shoes. 'Single-use' consumer goods are consumed immediately, for example an ice-cream.

Consumer durables yield utility over a longer time period, for example a refrigerator or washing machine . The utility received is not from the good itself but from the stream of services it yields over its lifetime.

Producer goods or **capital goods** do not directly satisfy wants, but do so indirectly. They are the plant and machinery acquired by firms for the purpose of producing other goods which may produce utility. As such they constitute the **assets** of firms and may be referred to as **capital assets**.

Services constitute intangible utilities, and may be further sub-divided into **personal services** and **commercial services**. Personal services satisfy needs through personal attention such as hairdressing, entertainment or medical treatment. Commercial services are not directly personal but act as aids to production, and include activities such as banking, insurance and communications.

7 The factors of production

The purpose of production is therefore to create utilities by providing a flow of goods and services to fulfil wants. In order to undertake production it is necessary to combine the resources available. These resources are known as the **factors of production**, and they can be combined in various proportions to produce economic goods. The factors of production can be classified as

- land
- labour
- capital

The activity of combining these factors of production is referred to as **enterprise**, which is sometimes included as a fourth factor of production. Enterprise is undertaken by the **entrepreneur** who accepts the **risk** of producing in advance of sale and in return receives **profit**, the rest of the revenue from sales going in payments to the other factors of production.

8 Choices

The problem of society forcing us to make choices is actually the problem of how to allocate existing resources to different uses and how to allocate the resulting goods and services to different members of society. Different societies may have different approaches to resolving these problems, but the problem remains the same everywhere. The three basic problems which all societies are forced to resolve can be expressed as **what, how** and **for whom**?

- **What?** – refers to the problem of which goods should be produced and in what quantities.
- **How?** – refers to the method of producing the goods, making the best use of available resources.
- **For whom?** – refers to the way in which the total output is to be distributed amongst the members of the community.

All economies face the same problems although their approach to solving them may differ.

9 Types of economy

There are basically three alternative approaches a society may adopt in order to solve the problems of what?, how? and for whom?, the **free market**, the **planned** (or **command**) **economy**, and the **mixed economy** although in reality it is more like a spectrum with differing degrees of mixture between the two extreme forms of a completely free market economy and a totally planned economy, with few examples of the extremes and most being at some intermediate point between the two extremes.

10 The free market

In a free market, or private enterprise economy, all the factors of production are owned by private individuals and the decisions of what, how, and for whom, are made unconsciously by the interaction of market forces. We must assume here that consumers are rational and always attempt to maximise the utility they receive from their incomes, and that entrepreneurs are also rational and always attempt to maximise their profits. Given these assumptions, consumers are free to purchase whatever they wish in the market place. This is sometimes expressed as 'consumer votes' in the sense that they will spend more of their incomes (votes) on goods they favour. As the demand for these goods increases their prices will rise, making them more profitable, and entrepreneurs seeking greater profit will respond by entering into production of these goods, thereby increasing their supply. Hence more of those goods for which consumers have expressed a preference are produced. Production is therefore said to respond to the 'price signals' which indicates those goods which should be produced, and **consumer sovereignty** is said to prevail over the market.

The technical problem of 'how to produce' is determined by competition between producers which forces each to adopt the least-cost method of production.

The problem of 'for whom', the problem of distribution, is determined by relative incomes, which in turn are determined by supply and demand in the markets for productive services. If labour is scarce relative to its demand then wages will be higher and a greater proportion of output will go to wage earners; the same is true of owners of land and capital.

The concept of consumer votes should not be equated with any concept of 'fairness' in the accepted sense; some people have far more 'votes' than others, and if this is seen as a problem then it is one of income distribution not the price mechanism in itself. (See Chapter 27 for more details on this).

We are now in a position to list the main advantages and disadvantages of the three main types of economy.

11 Strengths of the free market economy

- Because goods are produced in accordance with consumers' preferences then society's resources are also allocated in line with the preferences of consumers.
- Because production responds automatically to the 'price signals' of the market, there is no need for the activities of thousands of manufacturers to be co-ordinated as this happens autonomously.
- Only those goods which are wanted by consumers are produced.
- People are free to spend their money in whichever way they choose.
- The free market economy offers the opportunity for those people with sufficient drive and initiative to enter production and create wealth.

12 Weaknesses of the free market economy

- Luxury goods for some may be produced before others have the basic necessities of life.
- During periodic recession valuable resources stand idle.
- The free market may not operate efficiently because of the existence of monopolies, and competition may therefore be lacking.
- Essential goods and services may not be provided or at least not be provided in sufficient quantities by the market. Some of these goods are referred to as 'merit goods' as they are thought to be so beneficial to society that they should be available to everybody. Others which are referred to as pure public goods, can only be adequately provided by government from tax revenue, for example defence.
- The free market does not allow for the 'social costs' of the entrepreneur's activities, e.g. pollution of the environment.

13 The planned economy

The **planned** (or **command**) **economy** is characterised by the collective ownership of the means of production and hence the price mechanism does not operate. The decisions of what, how and for whom are made by a central planning body who make their decisions in view of what they perceive as the needs of society.

14 Strengths of the planned economy

- Necessities for everybody will be produced in advance of luxuries.
- Resources need not stand idle during recession.
- Goods can be distributed according to need rather than income.
- Social costs and benefits can be incorporated into the decision making process.

15 Weaknesses of the planned economy

- The problem of co-ordinating thousands of different production decisions in the absence of price signals. For example, the decision to build 5,000 tractors will require the co-ordination of the production of hundreds of thousands of components, and an incorrect decision can hold up the production of the whole 5,000.
- Goods may be produced which consumers do not want, or goods may not be produced in sufficient quantities, the result being shortages of some goods and surpluses of others.
- The lack of personal involvement may result in a lack of incentive.
- The central planning body develops bureaucratic self interest and becomes insensitive to those it is supposed to be serving.

16 The mixed economy

The **mixed economy** is characteristic of most modern economies, and whilst leaving much production in private hands it allows for a substantial role for the government in the production of certain goods and services, and controls the worst excesses of the market place. To some extent it attempts to gain the better aspects of both the previous systems. Today the concept of the mixed economy is generally accepted by UK governments although there may be disagreement over the extent of the government's role. The Conservative government, which came to power in 1979, made attempts to reduce the role of the state in the economy by 'privatising' some sectors of production and reducing the amount of intervention elsewhere.

The advantages and disadvantages are not listed here as they are self-evident from the advantages and disadvantages of the previous two, but we have listed here the main reasons for the involvement of the government in the mixed economy.

- To provide those essential goods and services which would **not be adequately provided by the free market**, in particular those referred to as **'merit goods'** such as education and health, or pure public goods such as defence.
- **Where market failure occurs,** i.e. monopoly; in order to protect the interests of the consumer and prevent the worst excesses of monopoly.
- **Where production, if left to the market, would be inefficient** due to duplication of plant and capacity, or if produced by large private monopolies would lead to excess

power over the consumer, e.g. electricity production and supply.

- **To maintain services** which are important both strategically and economically and which may otherwise be in danger of collapse, e.g. Railways, Rolls Royce Aero Engines.
- **To regulate the activities** of the private entrepreneur to prevent the worst aspects of private production, e.g. environmental pollution.
- **To regulate the economy** in order to maintain the level of demand, employment, balance of payments and inflation. The simultaneous control of each of these variables is difficult and they may in fact conflict, different governments emphasising the importance of different variables; however, most government involvement in the economy is aimed at the control of one or more of these macro-economic variables.

As an act of political belief governments may assume ownership over some areas of the economy. Generally, Labour governments tend to favour the extension of the role of the state by nationalisation, whilst Conservative governments prefer a less interventionist role. Although when threatened with massive job losses through the loss of a firm at the forefront of technological development and a major exporter, in the form of Rolls Royce Aero Engines Division, the Conservative government took it under the control of the public sector. Nationalisation may therefore be just as likely to occur as a result of economic and political expediency as of political dogma. As mentioned above, the Conservative government elected to office in 1979 was more strongly in favour of the private market than other recent governments and has undertaken the sale of many state assets in order to return them to the control of the private sector, in the belief that they would be operated more efficiently and require less support from the taxpayer.

17 Privatisation

The sale of state owned industries to the private sector is referred to as **privatisation**. In several instances this privatisation of state industries has been considered by many to be a highly radical move with the actual and proposed transfer to the private sector some industries which were formerly believed to be natural state monopolies (see Chapter 27) such as telephones and electricity. The main aims of the policy of privatisation are as follows.

- To improve the efficiency of the industries involved by exposing them to the competitive forces of the market.
- To make the industries less bureaucratic and more responsive to the wishes of the consumer and in turn more accountable for their own performance.
- To reduce the amount of government borrowing (public sector borrowing requirement) which was necessary to finance the deficits of many of the state industries. Over recent years privatisation has also proved to be an important source of revenue for the government. Table 1.1 lists the industries privatised since 1980.

The Trustee Savings Bank although not strictly a state industry was also sold to the private sector. The most controversial privatisations are of those public utilities such as electricity, gas and water which were previously considered as natural monopolies best maintained under state control so that they could be operated in the interest of the consumers. How they perform in the private sector will be evident in the course of time.

Table 1.1 Nationalised industries privatised 1980–96	
1980	Britoil
1982	Amersham International
1983	British Aerospace
	Associated British Ports
	Cable and Wireless
1984	British Telecom
	Jaguar Cars
1986	British Gas
1987	British Airways
1987	British Petroleum
1987	British Airports Authority
1987	Rolls Royce
1988	British Steel
1989	Water supply industry
1990	Electricity supply
1991	Electricity – regional boards
1992	PSA
1994	British Coal
	Railtrack
1995/ 1996	Rail franchises

Self assessment questions

1 Why might 'merit goods' not be provided in sufficient quantities by a free market economy?

2 Why is the statement 'a free market economy is better than a planned economy' by itself a 'value judgement'.

3 Give an example of a 'social cost' resulting from private production.

4 Explain what is meant by 'privatisation'.

2

Production

1 Sectors of production

As a starting point for considering the act of producing goods, or **production**, it is useful to sub-divide production into three broad categories:

- The **extractive** (primary) industries, refers to organisations involved in the extraction of basic (primary) materials, and includes industries such as mining, quarrying, farming, forestry and fishing. The outputs of these industries frequently form the raw materials inputs for other industries.
- The **manufacturing** (secondary) industries, are involved in the processing of materials or assembling of components to produce goods such as cars, food, chemicals, and engineering equipment.
- The **distributive** industries complete the chain of production by distributing the finished goods through the channels of distribution, through the wholesaler to the retailer and to the final consumer.

These industries however cannot operate effectively without the assistance of another sector of industry, the service industries.

2 The service industries

The service industries provide essential aids to those involved in production and include banking and insurance, advertising, general administration, transport and communications.

The UK economy has large numbers of people employed in each of these categories, Table 2.1 showing the size of the labour force in each sector and recent employment trends.

A characteristic of the UK economy in recent years has been the relative decline in the importance of manufacturing industry and the growth of the service sector. Figure 2.1 illustrates the percentage change in employment for each sector between 1955 and 1996.

Table 2.1						
	Employees 000's				**Changes 1971–1996**	
	1971	**1979**	**1986**	**1996**	**000's**	**% Change**
All industries & services	22 138	23 173	21 594	22 156	+16	+0.07
Agricultural, forestry and fishing	450	380	329	278	−172	−38.2
Manufacturing	8065	7253	5239	4015	−4050	−50.2
Construction	1198	1238	992	825	−373	−31.2
Energy and water supply	798	722	539	208	−590	−73.9
Service industries	11 627	13 580	14 495	16 830	+5203	+44.75

Civilian employment (excluding self-employment) in Great Britain, 1955 and 1996

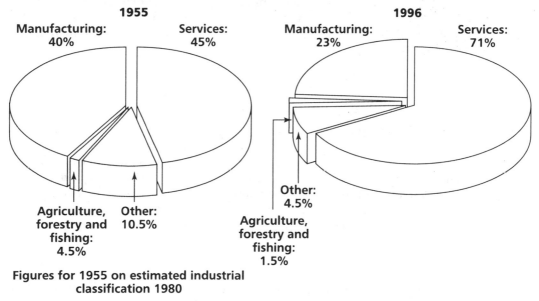

Figure 2.1 Civilian employment (excluding self-employment) in Great Britain, 1955 and 1996

3 The firm

When we refer to the **firm** or **enterprise** we refer to the unit of ownership or control. A firm may consist of an individual unit or a parent company with several subsidiary firms. An **industry** is usually defined according to the physical and technical characteristics of the output produced and consists of all the firms producing those goods.

4 Factors of production

As mentioned in Chapter 1 the **factors of production** are essential for production to take place. They can be combined in various proportions, according to their relative prices, in order to achieve the least-cost combination. The least-cost combination will however change over time as factor prices change according to their demand and supply, and also with changes in technology. It is however not only the quantity of a factor of production which is important but also its quality. We will next consider each of these factors more closely.

5 Land

Land in this context is a wider concept than its everyday meaning, and includes all the natural resources available to man which can be utilised for productive purposes and which are provided freely by nature. It therefore includes building land, farming land, minerals, rivers and seas.

The supply of land is of course relatively fixed, the important point in the study of economics however, is that land can be used for different purposes. Land can be transferred between different agricultural uses or from agricultural to building, and will tend to be transferred to that use where it can earn the greatest yield (income). The location of land cannot be changed however and this is particularly important in town centres where land may have a high site value, no matter how much the demand for such sites increases the supply cannot be increased and such sites may earn what is known as **economic rent** (See Chapter 21).

6 Labour

In order to produce goods the entrepreneur will need to hire the services of labour in return for a wage. As a productive resource both the quality and quantity of labour are important. The quantity of labour will depend upon factors such as the birth rate, average age of the population, total population size and the number of hours worked. Labour quality is an important factor in productivity and this is dependent upon education, training, the possession of appropriate skills, willingness to accept changes in working practices, and the extent to which the labour force is motivated. Also important are its aptitude and intelligence, its willingness to acquire new skills and to adapt to new technology.

7 Capital

Capital should not be confused with money. Capital is anything which is created, not for its own use but for the purpose of further production. It therefore has the effect of making the process of production less direct, in that labour utilises capital equipment in the act of production.

Capital can be subdivided into two types, working capital and fixed capital. Working capital is used up during the course of production and consists of stocks of raw materials, work in progress, and finished goods. Fixed capital is not used up in the production process but is retained within the organisation and includes premises, machinery, fixtures and fittings, and vehicles. Another way to consider it is that working capital consists of items acquired for the purpose of re-sale whilst fixed capital consists of items not bought for re-sale but retention within the business. Items of capital are generally referred to as **capital assets**.

The nation's stock of capital can be sub-divided into social capital, private and public sector industrial capital and private industrial capital. Table 2.2 identifies these with examples.

Table 2.2 Capital stock			
Private individual capital	**Private sector industrial capital**	**Public sector industrial capital**	**Social capital**
E.g. Housing stock.	E.g. Factories, . machines, equipment	E.g. Nationalised industries.	E.g. Schools, hospitals, roads.

Capital goods can only be created by foregoing **current consumption**, i.e. **saving**. Current consumption is foregone in order to increase **future consumption**. However merely the act of saving will not create a capital good, the saved resources must be utilised in order to create a **capital good**.

The creation of a capital good is often illustrated by reference to Robinson Crusoe on his desert island. He catches 5 fish each day by using a line. He decided to spend three days constructing a net. After constructing the net he can now catch 5 fish in one hour and spend the rest of his time growing other foodstuffs and enjoying a more interesting diet. The cost of his net was the 15 fish he did not catch whilst constructing the net. He had to forego present consumption in order to create a capital good which enabled him to have a higher level of future consumption.

8 Investment and depreciation

During the act of production each year some of the stock of capital is used up, i.e. machines wear out. This is referred to as **depreciation**. The total amount of capital produced each year is referred to as **gross investment**, and any addition to the stock of capital as **net investment**. Thus the act of just replacing worn out capital will not increase the stock of capital, so there can be gross investment without net investment, but only net investment will increase the productive capacity of the economy.
therefore

Gross investment – Depreciation = Net investment

9 Production possibility curves

We can usefully illustrate both the problem of scarcity and choice, of which the conflict between current consumption and capital formation is a prime example, by the use of **production possibility curves** (PPC).

In order to illustrate the concept we will assume that our economy is capable of producing two goods, good X and good Y. It has the choice of devoting all its resources to the production of good X and having none of good Y, devoting all its resources to good Y and having none of good X, or choosing some intermediate point and having some of both. This is illustrated in Figure 2.2. At point A society is producing all good Y and none of X, and at point B all of X and none of Y. At point C some of both are produced. Note that the shape of the PPC is concave to the origin; this is because as we move along the curve from A toward B and factors of production are transferred from the production of one good to the other, as successive units of the factors of production are transferred they will be less and less efficient in their new use due to **diminishing returns**, and for each unit of Y sacrificed we will gain smaller and smaller quantities of X, i.e. the opportunity cost increases. This illustrates that in an economy which is fully utilising its resources **substitution** is inevitable, and wherever there are scarce resources society must always make choices. At point U society's resources are under-utilised and we can have more of both goods by moving on to the PPC. Point Z is unobtainable and can only be achieved by a shift of the whole curve upwards and outwards; this can only occur as a result of technological change, increased productivity or an increase in available resources.

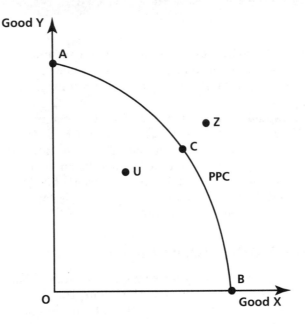

Figure 2.2

Figure 2.3 illustrates a society which in the current time period (t) has chosen a high level of consumption and a low level of production of capital goods.

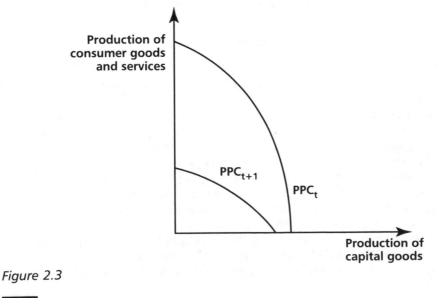

Figure 2.3

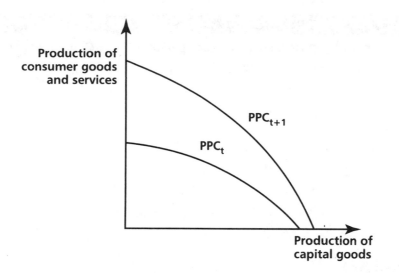

Figure 2.4

In the next time period (t + 1) the PPC has shifted towards the origin to PPC$_{t+1}$ producing less of both goods and therefore a lower standard of living. Figure 2.4 illustrates a society which in the current time period has chosen to have a high level of production of capital goods and a relatively lower level of production of consumer goods for current consumption. In the next time period (t + 1) however, the PPC has shifted outwards to PPC$_{t+1}$ and is enjoying a higher level of consumption and a high level of capital formation – by foregoing some current consumption they enjoyed a higher future 'standard of living'.

10 Diminishing returns

It cannot be assumed however that because we have more of a factor available we can always gain proportionate increases in output, as inevitably the returns from additional units of factors of production will tend to decline. This is referred to as the **law of diminishing returns** or **declining marginal productivity**. This states that as we add additional units of a variable factor to a constant factor then the product (output) of the variable factor will first of all rise but will eventually start to decline.

The theory assumes that all the units of the variable factor are identical in terms of productivity, and the techniques of production remain unchanged. In Table 2.4 **total product** refers to the total output of the variable factor, in this case labour. **marginal product** refers to the increase in Total Product from each additional unit of labour, and

$$\text{Average product} = \frac{\text{total product}}{\text{quantity of labour}}$$

In Table 2.3 we illustrate the example of a smallholder with one acre of land growing potatoes employing at first a single unit of labour and then employing more and more

Table 2.3			
Labour	Total product (Tonnes)	Average product (AP)	Marginal product (MP)
1	2	2	
2	10	5	8
3	21	7	11
4	36	9	15
5	55	11	19
6	63	10½	8
7	70	10	7
8	72	9	2
9	72	8	0

labourers and keeping the amount of land constant. This is represented graphically in Figure 2.5.

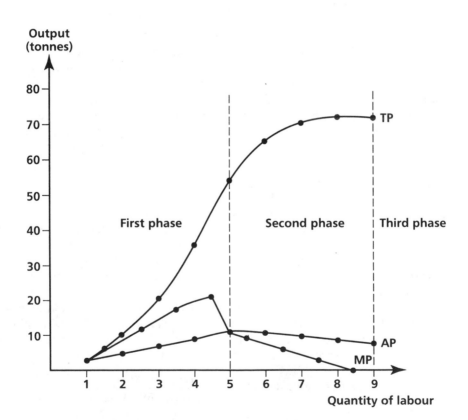

Figure 2.5

During the first phase as additional labour is added to the fixed factor (land) each successive unit raises output and total product (**TP**), marginal product (**MP**) and average product (**AP**) are all rising. This continues until the fifth man is added when MP reaches a peak and falls sharply cutting AP at its highest point after which AP also declines. During the second phase, after the addition of the fifth unit of labour, the **rate of growth** of TP declines and both AP and MP decline, MP declining more sharply than AP. Up to the fifth man total product increases at an **increasing rate** and there are **increasing returns**. After the fifth man the rate of growth of total product declines and **diminishing returns** set in as the marginal product declines. In the third phase at the point where total product begins to fall, after the ninth man, marginal product becomes negative.

The normal relationship between marginal product and average product is illustrated more clearly in Figure 2.6.

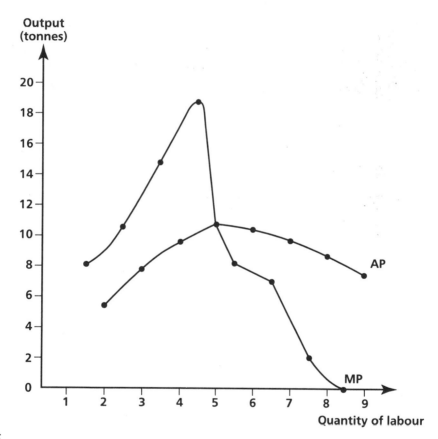

Figure 2.6

The law of declining marginal productivity assumes that one factor, in this case land, is held constant. In the long run however all the factors of production can be varied so the law of declining marginal productivity is really applicable to the short-run. Over the long run it is possible to increase the amount of land available or labour efficiency can be improved through training or improved equipment. In this way the effect of diminishing returns can be offset. This would represent a change in the **scale of production** and is dealt with later. The law of diminishing returns has important implications for the costs of production and will be referred to again later.

Self assessment questions

1 Distinguish between gross and net investment.
2 How is a capital good created?
3 What is meant by 'the law of diminishing returns'?
4 Identify the factors of production.
5 Why is the production possibility curve concave in shape?
6 How did the structure of employment in the UK change between 1955 and 1996?

3

Specialisation and the division of labour

1 Subsistence living

In a primitive society where individuals attempt to produce all their own requirements for living, life will be very basic and is referred to as **subsistence** living. Output will be very low and each individual will be producing just sufficient to survive. Each individual will be attempting to do their own hunting, fishing, building shelter, farming and making utensils and other requirements. Such production is extremely inefficient as an individual person is unlikely to possess equal talents in each of these activities; they may be good at some and very poor at others. It also means that they must be continually changing from one task to another or leaving some tasks whilst another one is completed.

2 Specialisation

The single most important element in allowing a society to advance economically is the act of **specialisation**. Specialisation occurs when each member of a society specialises in that task at which they are most talented. If each individual does this they become more productive and total output is increased. The person who is good at hunting devotes all their time to hunting, the person who is skilled at making bows and arrows makes them all the time. Each person now however produces a **surplus** over and above their own requirements, and the essential point is that they can **trade** this surplus for those goods which they do not produce.

3 Comparative advantage

The gains from specialisation can be achieved even if one person is better at all activities than another, provided one specialises in the activity in which they are most efficient and the other in the activity in which he or she is least inefficient. This is referred to as the principle of **comparative advantage**. If a person is better at all activities they are said to have an **absolute advantage** but they may still have a **greater comparative advantage** in the production of some goods and another person will have the **least comparative disadvantage** in the production of others. To illustrate this point, imagine there are two persons, A and B, both of whom manufacture pans and earthenware pots. Their output per day assuming they both divide their time equally is as follows:

A manufactures	either 40 pans or 40 pots per day.
B manufactures	either 37 pans or 16 pots per day.

Prior to specialisation actual output per day is:

A manufactures	20 pans and	20 pots per day
B manufactures	15 pans and	8 pots per day
Total output:	35 pans and	28 pots per day

Note that A is more efficient at producing both but is comparatively more efficient at producing pots, i.e. 40:16, whilst B is least inefficient at pans, i.e. 40:37. As a result, specialisation will raise total output.

After each specialising in the task at which they are most efficient, output per day is as follows:

A manufactures	0 pans and	40 pots
B manufactures	37 pans and	0 pots
Total output	37 pans	40 pots per day

Total output has increased by 2 pans and 12 pots per day.

Specialisation is not only the key to how society can raise its output and therefore its standard of living, but is also the precursor of trade.

4 The division of labour

Division of labour refers to the practice of breaking a complex task down into a number of simpler tasks and an individual can then specialise in one of these simple tasks. This is specialisation as most of us know it today in a factory setting where complex tasks, such as building a motor car, are broken down into many thousands of simple tasks, and individual workers specialise in one of them. Specialisation here is a narrower concept with the worker being used where he is most productive rather than most skilled.

A frequently quoted, but nevertheless relevant example, is the observation of a pin factory by the 18th century economist Adam Smith. He noted that the practice of making pins had been broken down into about 18 different operations: one man drawing out the wire, another cutting it, another putting points on, another grinding the heads, another fitting the heads, and so on. The output per head of the factory was about 5,000 pins per day, whereas if each person had to make the whole pin, Smith estimated that output would have been no more than a few dozen pins per day.

Specialisation and division of labour also occurs with the management functions of a business. As a firm grows it becomes impossible for a single person to have the necessary knowledge of all the functions, and to attempt to perform all of them, it would be extremely inefficient and time consuming. The firm will therefore employ specialists such as accountants, sales managers, engineers, buyers, production managers, and so on.

5 Mass production

Once division of labour has taken place and a process has been broken down into a number of simple tasks, it becomes easier to apply machines to the tasks. Machines can generally only perform a single task, i.e. they are inflexible, however when the process is broken down into its component tasks, machines can be applied more easily. This is the way in which **mass production** is facilitated.

The process of mass production, which carries specialisation and division of labour to its extreme, can be illustrated by reference to one of the earliest examples. Prior to the end of the 18th century muskets had always been individually produced by craftsmen who produced all the components and assembled them. All the components were unique and would fit only one weapon. At the end of the 18th century Eli Whitney received the contract from the new American government to produce muskets for the American Army, and was given a year to produce them. Until a few weeks before the delivery was due he had not produced a single weapon; he had in fact been producing the tooling – jigs, dies, stamping machines and setting out the work flow in his workshop. He was then able to produce them within a couple of weeks and fulfil his contract. After that of course he was then able to produce them more quickly and efficiently than anybody else.

Not only did this method produce the muskets more quickly and cheaply, but had a further advantage: all the components would fit any musket as they were identical, i.e. they were **interchangeable** or **standardised**, which meant that assembly was faster, and also that spare parts were available.

This method of production was later developed further by Henry Ford in America, who was the first manufacturer of motor cars to utilise mass production methods with the Model T, which was produced so cheaply and quickly that it became the most popular car in America for nearly 20 years and made the possibility of car ownership a reality for millions of low income Americans.

In recent years mass production has taken a further step forward with the increased use of micro-technology and robotics in assembly processes.

6 The advantages of specialisation

The advantage of specialisation is the productivity gain, which results from the following:

- People rapidly acquire skills when repeatedly performing a simple task.
- Training times and costs are reduced when skills are narrow.
- There is no waiting, or 'queuing' time; waiting for machines to become available.
- Time is not wasted moving around the workshop to perform different operations.
- It enables people to perform those tasks at which they have most natural aptitude.
- It facilitates the use of machinery, as machinery is easier to apply to a simple task.

7 The disadvantages of specialisation

There are, however, a number of disadvantages to the process:

- Consistently performing routine tasks soon becomes tedious and boring.
- Specialisation tends to remove the skill from work, hence workers are not given the opportunity to take a 'pride in their work'.
- A combination of the two disadvantages above tends to lead to 'alienation' and as a

result poor industrial relations. Workers will tend to lack motivation.

- A narrow specialisation may result in an increased risk of unemployment, and if the whole of the industry is in a recession it may be difficult to find employment. Also skills may become technically obsolete, e.g. typesetters in the newspaper industry.
- Where specialisation is taken to extreme, factories themselves tend to specialise, e.g. component manufacturers for the car industry. As a result the whole of industry becomes more interdependent, and is vulnerable to a breakdown of any part of the complex chain of production.

8 Barter

As mentioned earlier, in Chapter 2, specialisation results in surplus production and therefore trade. Early trade took the form of barter, where goods were simply 'swapped' for other goods. Barter has a number of weaknesses, however, which make it difficult for an economy to develop.

Goods are **non divisible** – if a bow is worth 2½ pots, we cannot trade as breaking a pot makes it worthless

If we want to trade not only do we need to find somebody who has what we want but they must also want what we have to give in exchange – a **double coincidence of wants**. The possibility of finding such a person is made greater the more people we meet, hence the development of market places where everyone can take their surplus goods and trade. This still happens in many parts of the world.

The weakness of barter leads to the next vital step in the development of an economy, **money**. Money facilitates the growth of trade and economic development.

9 Money

Money overcomes the weakness of barter because it has the advantage of being:

- Divisible
- Generally acceptable

Hence the problems of divisibility and double coincidence of wants are solved. Anybody will accept money and it can be divided into many denominations. Money can in fact be any commodity, and historically cowrie shells, salt, dogs' teeth (New Guinea) and wampum beads (Red Indians), have all been used. The easiest way to ensure general acceptability of a monetary unit is to ensure that it has intrinsic value, hence the popularity of gold coins for so long. We now use paper money which has no intrinsic value, but whose acceptability is based purely on people's confidence. That part of the note issue based on nothing other than people's confidence is known as the **fiduciary issue**. Bank accounts also function as money. The characteristics needed by a commodity for it to function as money are:

- **Generally acceptable**
- **Homogeneous (same)**
- **Divisible**
- **Portable**
- **Scarce**
- **Durable**

In this context it is interesting to consider cigarettes, which functioned very efficiently as money in prisoner-of-war camps.

The functions of money can be stated briefly as follows:

- **A medium of exchange**.
- **A measure of value** – the goods can be expressed in terms of a standardised unit.
- **A store of value** – it is a convenient form in which to store wealth.
- **A method of deferring payments** – it facilitates the system of trade credit.

Money has further significance relating to production. The development of money makes wage payments possible; it therefore becomes possible to concentrate the production process into factories where specialisation and division of labour can be carried further, into the system of mass production.

10 The limits of specialisation

The limits to which specialisation and mass production can be carried are set by:

- The extent of the development of the monetary system.
- The size of the market.

In order to offset the limiting effect of market size countries may join large trading blocks such as the EU, or as in the case of Britain in the 19th century, by trading with an Empire, or by trying to export throughout the world as does Japan today.

Specialisation and division of labour are the pre-requisites for economic development and not surprisingly were described by Adam Smith as 'the source of the wealth of nations'.

Self assessment questions

1 Why does specialisation and division of labour raise output?

2 What are the disadvantages of specialisation and division of labour?

3 Why is barter inefficient?

4 What are the characteristics of money?

5 What limits the extent of specialisation and division of labour?

6 Discuss the links between specialisation, division of labour and mass production.

7 How does specialisation take place in a mass production factory system?

Elements of demand

1 Market price

We consider next the factors determining market prices. Price, it should be noted, is not the same as value. Value is a subjective evaluation and is not necessarily the same as the price we receive for an item in exchange. We may place a value on an item for a variety of reasons, such as sentiment, but here we are interested only in the value the market places on a good which can conveniently be measured by its price. Market prices are determined by the forces of **demand** and **supply**.

2 Effective demand

When we refer to **demand** in economics we are referring to **effective demand**, not how much people would like to purchase but how much they can afford and are willing to buy at each price. Demand is, then, the quantity of a good demanded by consumers at a price in a particular time period.

3 Demand curves

At any period of time we can identify a definite relationship between the market prices and the quantity demanded of a good This can be referred to as a **demand schedule**. In Table 4.1 we illustrate a demand schedule for potatoes.

Table 4.1 market demand schedule for potatoes	
(1) price (£s per tonne)	**(2) quantity demanded (000 tonnes per month)**
30	25
20	50
15	75
10	125
5	200

Figure 4.1 is referred to as a **demand curve**, identified by the letters DD. From it we can read off the quantities demanded at each price. Note that as the price rises the quantity demanded falls and vice versa, the relationship between price and quantity demanded is therefore an **inverse relationship**. It is essential to note at this stage that changes in the quantity demanded, or movements along the demand curve occur as a result of **changes in price only**, all other factors remaining constant, i.e. it is an example of the ceteris paribus rule.

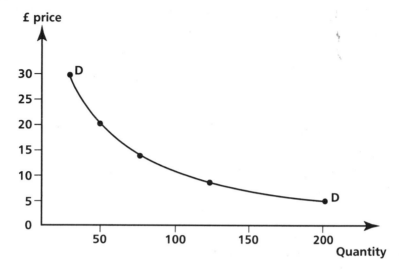

Figure 4.1

In Figure 4.2 a rise in the price of potatoes causes a movement along the curve, hence the rise in price to £20 reduces the quantity demanded to 50, a fall in the price increases the quantity demanded to 125. Changes in the quantity demanded may also be referred to as **extensions** or **contractions** in demand.

Figure 4.2

If other factors do change, i.e. the **conditions of demand**, then there is a shift of the whole demand curve. For example, supposing that there is a substantial increase in incomes so people buy more meat and less potato, this will cause a change in demand in that less will be demanded at each price. This change in the **conditions of demand** is represented in Figure 4.3 by a **shift** of the whole demand curve downwards and to the left, to D"D", and at the price of £15 instead of 75 being demanded, only 50 are demanded. An increase in demand is represented by a **shift** of the whole curve upwards and to the right to D'D' with 130 now being demanded at price 15 as a result of a favourable change in the conditions of demand; the same is true at each price, as essentially there is now a new demand curve.

Figure 4.3

4 Summary

A change in the **quantity demanded** (or a **contraction** or **extension of demand**) is represented by a **movement along the demand curve**.

A **change in demand** occurs when the change occurs in the conditions of demand and are a result of **factors other than price**.

Changes in demand can occur as a result of:

- Changes in the price of a substitute good (see 7).
- Changes in the price of a complementary good (see 7).
- Changes in tastes or fashion.
- A change in incomes.
- Advertising.

5 Income and substitution effects

Demand curves are nearly always drawn as sloping downwards from left to right, consequently we refer to the **law of downward sloping demand**.
Demand curves slope downwards because:

- As the price of a good falls it becomes available to more people with lower income levels.
- As the price of a commodity falls it will be substituted for other commodities which have become relatively more expensive (substitution effect).
- As the price of a commodity falls it increases the **real income** of the consumer who can then buy more of all goods (income effect).
- As we obtain more of a good the additional utility (satisfaction) we receive from the extra units consumed tends to decline, we will therefore value it less highly and will only be prepared to buy it at a lower price. This is referred to as the law of **diminishing marginal utility**.

6 Marginal utility

Although there have been many attempts to measure utility it remains a subjective concept. To illustrate the concept, imagine a consumer who had not had a bar of chocolate for many years; if he now received a chocolate bar he would enjoy a high level of satisfaction, or utility, from it and would therefore value it highly in terms of price. If he now received a second bar he would receive more utility but not as much as from the first; his **total** utility is increasing, but his **marginal** utility is declining, and he will place a lower value on the second and subsequent bars than on the first. Eventually he may feel quite ill from consuming chocolate and place no value at all on further bars. Figure 4.4 illustrates the marginal utility from each additional bar of chocolate declining whilst total utility increases at a declining rate. In Figure 4.5 the marginal units are plotted separately and the smooth line A-B drawn through them is identical to a demand curve. The concept of diminishing marginal utility underlies the slope of the demand curve and is useful in explaining other aspects of consumer behaviour.

7 Substitutes and complements

Not all goods are completely independent in demand and the change in the price of one good may affect the demand for other goods.

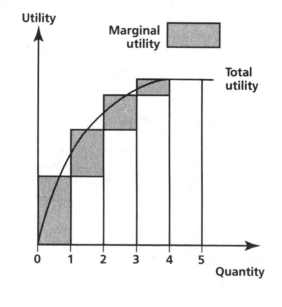

Figure 4.4

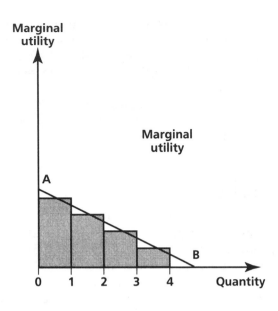

Figure 4.5

Substitute goods (competitive demand). An example of a substitute good is margarine and butter. Margarine (the **inferior good**) will be substituted for butter (the **normal good**) if the price of butter rises and vice versa if the price of butter falls. When the price of coffee doubled after the crop failure in 1976, there was a substantial increase in the demand for tea.

Complementary goods (joint demand). These are goods which normally go together such as shoes and laces, cars and tyres, bread and butter.

We can summarise the effect of changes in one of the two goods as follows:

- A rise in the price of a good will result in a fall in the demand for that good and an increase in the demand for its substitute. A fall in the price of a good will reduce the demand for its substitute.
- A rise in the price of a good will result in a fall in the demand for that good and therefore a reduction in the demand for its complement. A fall in the price of a good will increase the demand for its complement.

8 Exceptional demand curves

There are a few exceptions to the law of downward sloping demand, which are sometimes referred to as **exceptional demand curves** or **regressive demand curves**.

Figure 4.6 illustrates the case of regression at the upper end of the curve and may occur with **goods of ostentation**, such as jewellery, antiques or paintings. An increase in the price from P to P' increases the quantity demanded from Q to Q'. People attribute status to such goods and if sold too cheaply people will not feel they are receiving something providing the necessary status. This has certainly been found to be the case with imitation jewellery and it is not uncommon for antiques dealers to find they can sell certain items more easily when the price is raised.

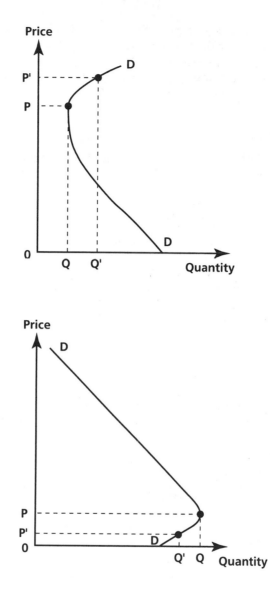

Figure 4.6

Figure 4.7

Commodity dealers who take a price increase as an indication of even higher prices in the future will increase the size of their current purchases in the hope of avoiding the highest prices.

Figure 4.7 indicates regression at the lower end of the curve. A price fall from P to P reduces the quantity demanded from Q to Q'. This may occur with certain inferior goods, in such cases these goods are referred to as '**Giffin Goods**'. When a high percentage of household income is spent on such goods, any substantial price reduction will increase household income and the additional income will be used to purchase more of the superior good and less will be bought of the inferior good, potatoes and meat being the classic example. It is in fact a case of the income effect outweighing the substitution effect.

Commodity buyers who take a price fall as an indication of even lower prices in the future will reduce the size of their current purchases hoping to re-enter the market when the price has reached its lowest point.

The vast majority of goods however follow the law of downward sloping demand and are referred to as **normal goods**.

9 Market demand

Each consumer has their own individual demand schedule and demand curve for the commodities they purchase, and in order to derive the market or industry demand, i.e. the total demand for the output of the commodity, we merely sum horizontally each individual's demand curve at each price.

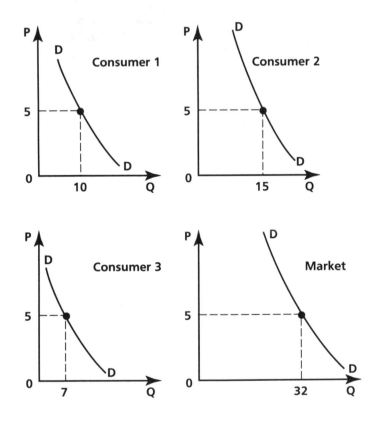

Figure 4.8

In Figure 4.8 each consumer's demand at price 5 is added to give one point on the market, or industry, demand curve. This can be done at every price to give a complete market demand curve. Market or industry demand curves always slope downwards because if the industry as a whole increases or lowers price, then the quantity demanded will decrease or increase. However, for each individual firm in the industry this may not be the case.

Self assessment questions

1 What is meant by 'effective demand'?

2 Why do demand curves generally slope downwards?

3 Distinguish between a movement along a demand curve and shift in a demand curve.

4 Give one example of an exception to the law of downward sloping demand.

5 What is meant by diminishing marginal utility?

6 Distinguish between an individual consumer's demand curve and a market demand curve.

7 What is meant by:

   (a) A substitute good;
   (b) Complementary good;
   (c) A good of ostentation?

Elements of supply

1 Supply

Supply refers to the quantity which a producer is willing and able to put on to the market at a particular price during a particular time period.

Supply is ultimately determined by cost and costs tend to rise as output is increased (see Chapter 9). If we imagine a farmer producing potatoes, if he is to expand output of potatoes he will first of all need to replace other crops, such as barley, with potatoes, which he will only be willing to do if the price of potatoes is sufficiently high to yield him a higher return than the alternative crop. If he wishes to expand output further he may need to utilise marginal land which is not normally used. Such land will require the application of more labour and fertiliser and will therefore be more expensive to cultivate; a higher price will therefore be required by the farmer before the use of such land is considered. The law of supply therefore, says that **more of a good will be supplied at a higher price than at a lower price**, cet. par.

2 Supply schedule

In order to illustrate the relationship between price and supply we will utilise the example of the quantity of potatoes a farmer is willing to put on the market at different prices, and Table 5.1 is an example of such a supply schedule.

Table 5.1 Supply schedule for potatoes	
(1) Price (£s per tonne)	(2) Quantity Supplied (000 tonnes per month)
30	150
20	100
15	75
10	50
5	0

3 Supply curve

By plotting the data we produce the **supply curve** as illustrated in Figure 5.1, identified by the letters SS. From it we can identify the quantity which will be supplied at each price. As the price rises the quantity supplied also rises. Note that the curve slopes upwards to the right and we therefore refer to the **law of upwards sloping supply**. Supply curves therefore in general slope upwards and to the right. Like the demand curve, the supply curve is drawn on the ceteris paribus assumption – that no factors other than price change. If other factors do change, then there is a shift of the whole supply curve.

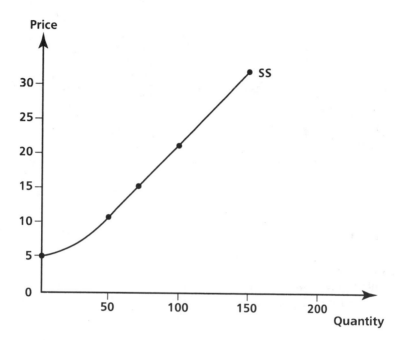

Figure 5.1

4 Movements along the supply curve

Movements along a supply curve occur in response to **price changes only** and are referred to as a change in the **quantity supplied** (or a **contraction or extension of supply**).

5 Changes in supply

A **change in supply** occurs when the change occurs in the conditions of supply and are a result of **factors other than price**.
Changes in supply can occur as a result of

- **Technical change**, i.e. changes in productivity as a result of technical innovation.
- **Changes in working practices.**
- **Weather** – important for natural commodities
- **Changes in taxes or subsidies.**
- **Changes in the prices of the factors of production affecting costs.**

6 Supply graphs

Figure 5.2 illustrates the effects of price changes on the quantity supplied, an increase in the price raising the quantity supplied and vice versa.

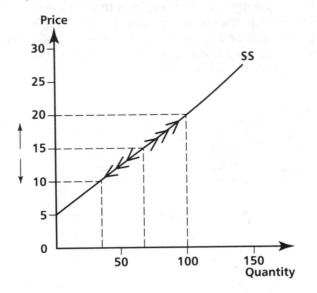

Figure 5.2

Figure 5.3 illustrates a change in supply, resulting from a change in the conditions of supply, represented by a shift in the whole supply curve. An **increase in supply** is repre-sented by a shift of the entire curve downwards to the right from SS to SS', with a greater quantity supplied at each and every price. A **reduction in supply** is represented by a shift of the entire curve upwards to the left, from SS to SS", with a smaller quantity supplied at each price.

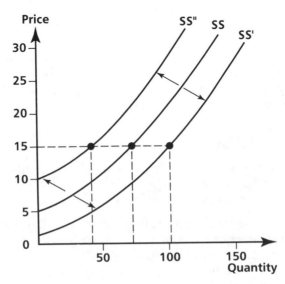

Figure 5.3

7 Joint supply

When some goods are produced it automatically results in the production of other goods, i.e. they are in **joint supply**. For example, an increase in beef production increases the supply of hides. An increase in the supply of petrol increases the supply of all oil derivatives produced in the refining process.

8 Exceptional supply

One exception to the law of upward sloping supply is the case of the backward sloping supply curve for labour, illustrated in Figure 5.4. An increase in the wage rate (the price of labour) from W to W' actually reduces the number of hours worked from Q to Q'. The supply curve is normal up to W then slopes backwards. This is because at higher wage rates some labour may prefer additional leisure to work once wages rise above W.

Most goods however follow the law of upward sloping supply.

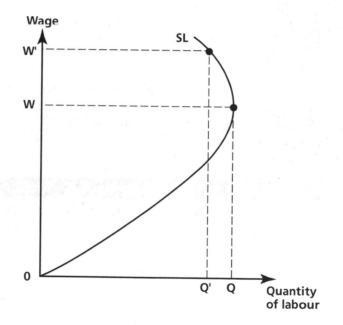

Figure 5.4

Self assessment questions

1 Why do supply curves slope upwards?
2 Distinguish between movements along a supply curve and a shift in the supply curve.
3 What effect would improved machinery have on the supply curve?
4 What effect would the abandonment of a restrictive labour practice have on the supply curve?
5 Under what circumstances could an increase in the wage rate reduce the supply of labour?

6

The determination of market price

1 Market prices

Having considered both demand and supply, we are now in a position to analyse the way in which market prices are determined.

The price of a commodity is determined jointly by the interaction of demand and supply. In order to illustrate this we can now combine the demand schedule (Table 4.1) and the supply schedule (Table 5.1) in Table 6.1 below.

TABLE 6.1 Combined supply and demand schedules for potatoes		
(1) Price (£s per tonne)	(2) Quantity demanded (000s tones per month)	(3) Quantity supplied (000s tonnes per month)
30	25	150
20	50	100
15	75	75
10	125	50
5	200	0

By plotting both the demand and supply curves on to a single graph we can obtain the market equilibrium price. Market equilibrium price is that price at which demand and supply are equal, and in Figure 6.1 can be seen to be the point where demand and supply curves intersect. It is generally referred to as the **equilibrium price (E)**, and here the equilibrium price is £15 with quantity 75. This can also be found by inspecting the demand and supply schedules for the price at which demand and supply are equal. At any price below £15 demand will exceed supply and shortages will result; at any price above £15 supply will exceed demand and there are surplus stocks on the market.

2 Market equilibrium

For further analysis of equilibrium price we will identify prices by using P and quantity by Q.

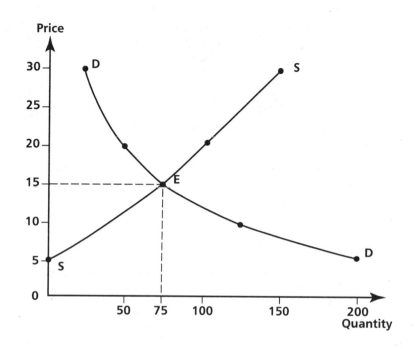

Figure 6.1

Market equilibrium price, or equilibrium price is therefore the price at which demand and supply are equal. Equilibrium price is the price at which the market will clear, i.e. the amount consumers are willing to buy is exactly the same as the amount suppliers will willingly supply: there are no shortages and no unsold stocks on the market. In Figure 6.2 demand and supply curves intersect at the equilibrium price Pe and quantity Qe. If at the commencement of the day's trading the price was set at P, there would be an excess of supply over demand and there would be an unsold surplus on the market of A–B. The only way in which these surplus stocks could be cleared would be to reduce the price, which would continue until the market equilibrium (E) was established, with demand and supply equal at price Pe and quantity Qe. If the price was set at P' demand would exceed supply by F–G and a shortage would prevail at that price. The excess demand would bid up prices and producers would respond by increasing supplies, which would continue until market equilibrium was achieved at price Pe and quantity Qe. Equilibrium price is therefore the **price to which a market will always return in the short run**, ceteris paribus.

This analysis of equilibrium price makes the 'ceteris paribus' assumption that all other factors remain unchanged, however over different time periods other factors may change resulting in different equilibrium prices. It is necessary next to examine more closely how changes in the factors underlying demand and supply may affect equilibrium prices.

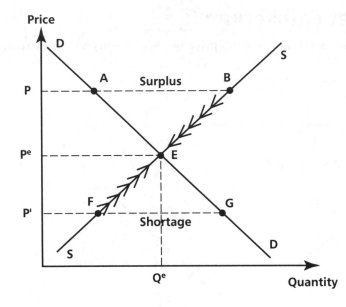

Figure 6.2

3 Changes in demand and supply

Figure 6.3 illustrates the market equilibrium for a good, for example butter, at price P and quantity Q. A substantial fall in the price of margarine would increase the demand for margarine and shift the demand curve for butter in the diagram downwards from D to D', with a equilibrium at E', a market price of P', and quantity Q'.

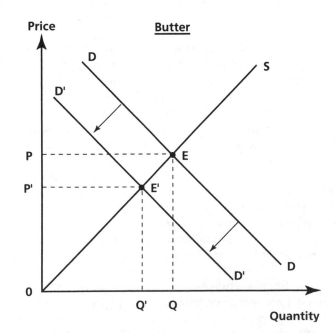

Figure 6.3

Less is now demanded at each price. A rise in the price of margarine would have caused a shift of the demand curve in the opposite direction, there would be an increase in the demand for butter as consumers' preferences switched to the commodity which had become relatively cheaper in order to maximise the utility they receive from their income. Similar shifts in demand can also be as a result of changes in consumers' tastes and preferences, for example if consumers became convinced that consuming too much butter was likely to be a health hazard. A similar shift from D to D' could also be the result of a heavy advertising campaign by the producers of margarine.

4 The interaction of markets

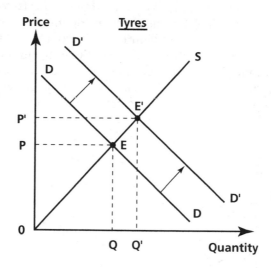

Figure 6.4

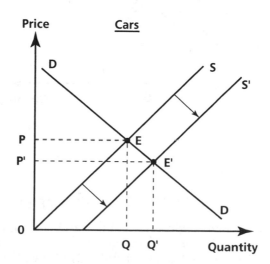

Figure 6.5

Figure 6.4 illustrates the market for tyres, and Figure 6.5 the market for cars, both of which are complementary goods. The car industry now introduces more productive technology such as 'robotics' which lower the costs of production, hence the supply curve shifts from S to S', and there is a movement along the demand curve DD to a new equilibrium at E', with lower price P and greater quantity Q'. As a result there is a change in the demand for tyres, with the demand curve shifting from DD to D'D', with higher price P' and quantity Q' with equilibrium at E'.

5 Partial equilibrium

Figure 6.4 can be referred to as a **partial equilibrium**. If the higher price P' persists for a substantial time period the tyre industry may attract more factors of production and become more productive, shifting the supply curve down to S' with new equilibrium at E'' with lower price P'' as illustrated in Figure 6.6. The final equilibrium price may even be lower than P. As the final equilibrium price in the long run after the factors of production have adapted to the new situation cannot be stated with certainty, it is said to be **indeterminate**: whilst the short run position in 6.6 can be stated with certainty and is said to be **determinate** which occurs before all factors of production have adjusted to the new market situation.

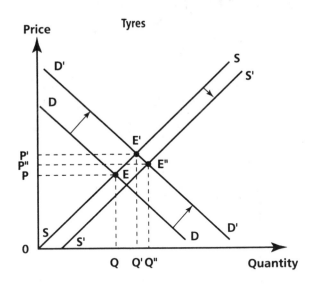

Figure 6.6

6 Applications of demand and supply analysis

In this section we consider some applications of demand and supply analysis.

If the government attempts to control rents and sets a rent ceiling of Rc below the market equilibrium E, then Q^0 will be demanded and only Q supplied leaving a shortage of rented accommodation of J–K.

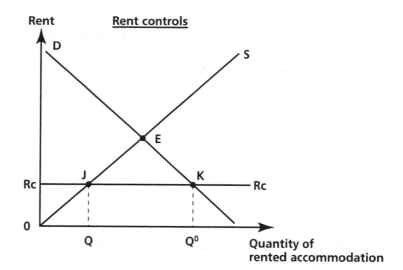

Figure 6.7

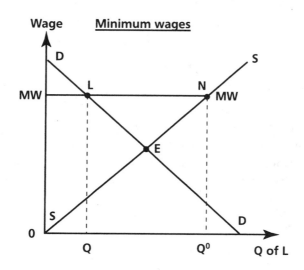

Figure 6.8

Attempts to force up wage levels by imposing a legal minimum wage, such as MW, results in a surplus of labour (more people wanting jobs than can obtain them at the pre-vailing wage rate). At MW, Q is demanded and Q^0 supplied, leaving a surplus of LN. An attempt was made in Costa Rica to raise wage rates in such a way with exactly the results predicted above.

In both cases there would have been no problem if the controls had been set so as to coincide with the market equilibrium price.

Figure 6.9 illustrates the attempt by a government to impose rationing.

As a result of an increase in demand from D to D' the equilibrium price rises to E'. The government attempts to control the price at CP, however at this price there is a shortage of EM. To achieve the ceiling price the government must reduce 'effective demand' back to DD by some form of rationing such as ration tickets. Even so some of the shortage will still be met illegally on 'black markets' at the market equilibrium, E' and price P'.

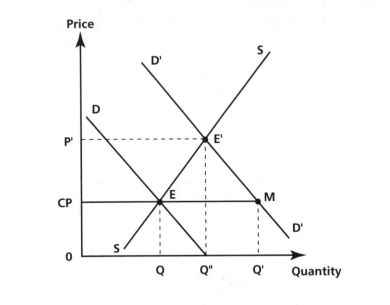

Figure 6.9

7 Taxation and the market

Incidence refers to who bears the burden of tax. Figure 6.10 illustrates the incidence of an indirect tax payable by a producer on each unit of sales. The tax is A–B, and shifts the supply curve upwards by the amount of the tax, but the price to the consumer increases by only P to P', i.e. C to E', whilst DC is absorbed by the producer. The amount which is passed on and the amount which is absorbed depends upon the relative demand and supply elasticities (see Chapter 7), in this case 50% each.

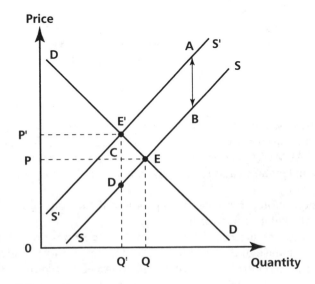

Figure 6.10

Self assessment questions

1 What is meant by 'equilibrium price'?

2 How does an increase in the firm's costs (cet. par.) affect equilibrium price?

3 What would be the effect of a legal minimum wage set below the equilibrium wage?

4 Distinguish between partial and full equilibrium.

5 Illustrate by the use of demand and supply diagrams the effect on the equilibrium price of coal of a substantial increase in the price of oil.

6 What is meant by 'the incidence of a tax'?

Elasticity

1 Total revenue

Total revenue (TR) refers to the firm's total receipts in monetary terms from its sales. It can be calculated therefore as **price × quantity**, i.e. TR = P × Q. This is also the area of the rectangle below the demand curve, shown as the shaded area in Figure 7.1.

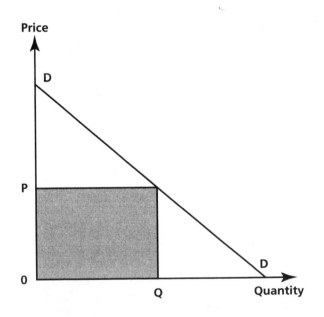

Figure 7.1

The area of this rectangle, and therefore TR will change as prices are changed, and of course firms will want this area of TR to be as large as possible. **Price elasticity of demand** (PED) refers to the way in which TR changes with variations in price.

2 Price elasticity of demand

Intuitively we can reason that a firm may reduce its price and by so doing sell so many extra units that its TR is increased, despite charging a slightly lower price per unit. Alternatively a firm may raise its price but in so doing lose so many units of sales that its TR declines. In both cases the opposite is also possible, i.e. reducing price may decrease TR, and in raising price TR may increase. This effect on TR of a price change is referred to as **price elasticity of demand (PED)**. A more precise definition is: **price elasticity of demand is the relationship between the proportionate (or percentage) change in price and the proportionate (or percentage) change in quantity demanded.**

3 Elastic and inelastic demand

Where the quantity demanded is highly responsive to price changes demand is said to be **elastic** and where it is unresponsive it is said to be **inelastic**. This can be illustrated by the use of demand curves, however with the exception of three 'special cases' **the slope of the demand curve is not a reliable guide to elasticity,** and extreme care should be taken in interpreting diagrams.

Figure 7.2 illustrates the concept of elastic demand over a given price range. A price reduction from £2.00 to £1.80 increases quantity demanded from 60 to 90, a 10% reduction in price has resulted in a 50% increase in demand, as a result TR has increased from £120 to £162. A price increase has the opposite effect and TR falls. Demand is very responsive to price changes in both directions over the price range £1.80–£2.

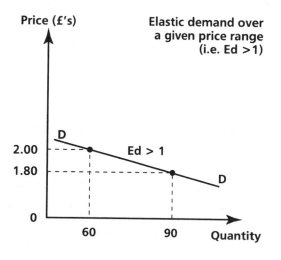

Figure 7.2

Figure 7.3 illustrates the concept of inelastic demand over a given price range. A price reduction from £2.00 to £1.50 increases the quantity demanded from 60 to 66, a 25% price reduction has resulted in an increase in quantity demanded of 10%, as a result TR has fallen from £120 to £99. A price increase has the opposite effect and TR increases. Demand is unresponsive to price changes in both directions. It is important to realise however that

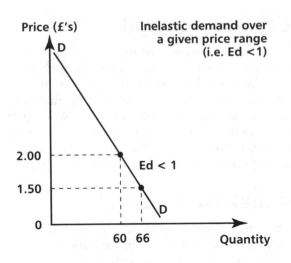

Figure 7.3

these diagrams only represent elasticity within the relevant part of the demand curve and in different parts of the demand curve elasticity will be different.

4 Visual interpretations

Visual comparisons of the elasticity of demand of two products can only be made when the following conditions apply:

- The scales are identical (note that in Figure 7.2 and 7.3 changing the scale changes the slope of the curve.
- Price changes are identical.
- The price at which the comparison is made is identical.

5 Measuring elasticity

Elasticity of demand, except in three 'limiting cases', varies at different points on the demand curve, and (except in the three special cases) there is no such thing as elastic or inelastic demand curves because measurements of elasticity are relative measures, which depend upon percentage changes taken at a particular point, whilst diagrams represent absolute changes. For this reason it is preferable to measure PED by the use of formulae. The formula which is most commonly used to measure PED is

$$\text{PED} = \frac{\textbf{percentage (or proportionate) change in quantity demanded}}{\textbf{percentage (or proportionate) change in price}}$$

For percentage changes this can be represented in notational form as

$$\text{PED} = \frac{\%\Delta Q}{\%\Delta P} \qquad \text{(where } \Delta = \text{a small change)}$$

The formula can also be represented as follows:

$$PED = \frac{\Delta Dx / Dx}{\Delta Px / Px}$$

Where:

ΔDx = the change in the quantity demanded of good x
Dx   = the original quantity demanded of good x
ΔPx = the change in the price of good x
Px   = the original price of good x.

The formula measures the degree of change in quantity demanded to a small change in price over a small area on a demand curve; and either percentage or proportionate changes can be used.

Table 7.1	
Price (P)	Quantity
6	100
5	200
4	300
3	400
2	500
1	600

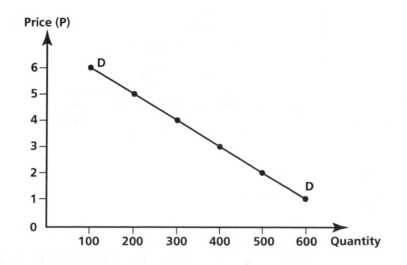

Figure 7.4

The resulting coefficient gives a measure of the degree of elasticity around a point on the demand curve. If it is < 1 demand is inelastic, > 1 demand is elastic, = 1 demand is unitary (see Figure 7.8) or 0 demand is totally inelastic (see Figure 7.6).

Table 7.1 is a simple demand schedule and Diagram 7.4 is its demand curve.

Using the formula to obtain an estimate of PED for a price reduction from 5p to 4p we have

$$PED = \frac{\%\Delta Q}{\%\Delta P} = \frac{100/200 \times 100}{1/5 \times 100} = \frac{50\%}{20\%} = 2.5$$

which represents a high degree of elasticity.

For a price reduction from 2p to lp we have

$$= \frac{100/500 \times 100}{1/2 \times 100} = \frac{20\%}{50\%} = 0.4$$

which represents an inelastic demand. This illustrates the fact that PED normally varies along a demand curve, and along a straight line demand curve will vary from 0 to ∞ (zero to infinity).

Figure 7.5 illustrates how a straight line demand curve passes from ∞ through an inelastic portion to the mid-point which is unitary, through an inelastic section to zero at the quantity axis.

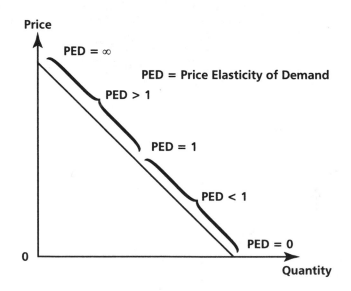

Figure 7.5

6 Extremes of PED

There are three special or 'limiting' cases of PED referred to earlier, and here the demand curve is a true representation of the PED

Figure 7.6 represents the case where PED = 0, quantity demanded will be totally unresponsive to price (within a relevant price range).

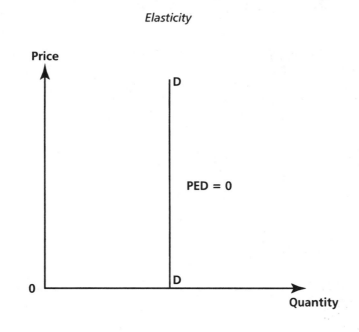

Figure 7.6

Figure 7.7 represents the case of the infinitely elastic demand curve PED = ∞ . Any increase in price will result in zero being demanded, any reduction in price will result in an infinitely large demand (this is the perfectly competitive case – see Chapter 14).

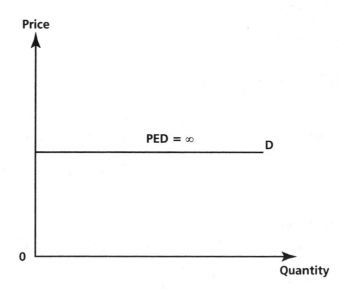

Figure 7.7

Figure 7.8 represents the unitary demand curve, PED = 1. As price is varied quantity demanded varies proportionately to maintain a constant TR. Mathematically it is a rectangular hyperbola.

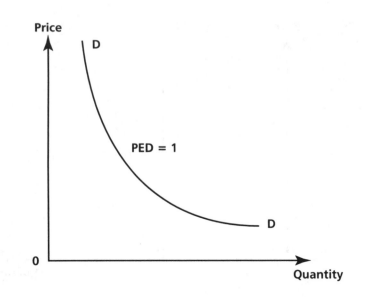

Figure 7.8

7 Determinants of PED

PED is determined by the following factors:

- The number and closeness of substitutes.
- The proportion of income the good accounts for.
- Whether the good is a necessity or a luxury.
- The influence of habit.

8 Applications of PED

An estimate of price elasticity of demand is an important element in a firm's pricing policy, particularly when it is considering price increases or reductions.

It is also important for the Chancellor of the Exchequer when selecting goods for the imposition of taxes or duties. It is preferable to select goods which are in inelastic demand in order to be certain of maintaining the tax revenue, e.g. petrol, spirits, beer and cigarettes.

9 Point elasticity

The measurement of elasticity used so far is referred to as **arc elasticity**. Arc elasticity measures the average value of elasticity over a small segment of a demand curve. An alternative measurement is **point elasticity** which measures elasticity at a single point on the demand curve and is therefore a more accurate measure, which unlike arc elasticity, is independent of the direction of the price change. The concept is illustrated in Figure 7.9, where point elasticity is given by the slope of the line A–B where it is tangential to the demand curve at the point under consideration, i.e. point x. The slope of the line A–B is given by $\Delta P / \Delta q$, therefore point elasticity can be defined as

$$PED = \frac{\Delta q/q}{\Delta P/P}$$

rearranging the terms gives

$$PED = \frac{\Delta q}{\Delta P} \cdot \frac{P}{q}$$

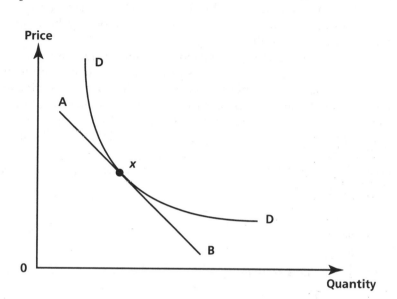

Figure 7.9

Where

P = original price
q = original quantity
Δq = an infinitely small change in quantity
ΔP = an infinitely small change in price

Point elasticity of demand therefore depends upon the slope of the demand curve, $\Delta q/\Delta P$ and the specific point on the demand curve at which elasticity is to be calculated, P/q. Those familiar with calculus will recognise that this process in fact amounts to using differentiation to find the rate of change of quantity with respect to price at a point on the demand curve. The smaller the changes taken in the calculation of arc elasticity the closer the result will be to the point elasticity value. In most instances, particularly for examination purposes, arc elasticity will be a sufficient measurement.

10 Income elasticity of demand (IED)

This measures the responsiveness of demand for a good to changes in income, and is calculated as

$$IED = \frac{\text{Percentage change in quantity demanded}}{\text{Percentage change in income}}$$

If the resulting coefficient for income elasticity of demand is greater than 1 then the good is **income elastic** and a rise in income would result in a **more than proportionate increase in quantity demanded**. This would be the case for all **normal goods**.

If income elasticity of demand is between 0 and 1 the good is said to be **income inelastic**, and a rise in income would result in a **less than proportionate rise in demand**. For example, there is a tendency for the demand for basic foodstuffs to rise less rapidly than income, referred to as **Engel's law.**

If income elasticity of demand is equal to 1 (unitary) the demand for the good **rises in exact proportion to the rise in income**. A positive relationship between income and demand would be expected for all normal goods.

The exceptions to the expected relationship between income and demand would be where income elasticity of demand = 0, i.e. a proportionate change in income results in no change in demand; and where income elasticity of demand is negative and increases in income result in a reduction in demand for the product, which would be the case for **inferior goods**, particularly those referred to earlier as Giffin goods. For example, as incomes grow, consumers may cease buying margarine and shift their buying preferences to butter.

The different measurements of income elasticity of demand can be represented graphically as in Figure 7.10 below.

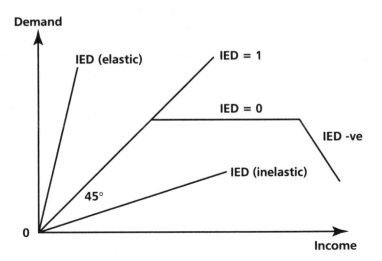

Figure 7.10

The concept of income elasticity of demand (IED) can be important for firms when forecasting the sale of their product during a period when incomes are changing. This can be illustrated with the simple example of a consumer good such as men's cotton shirts. In Figure 7.11 the pattern of demand for cotton shirts as income rises can be seen to pass through four phases. In phase A, income is too low for the purchase of cotton shirts and the consumer is restricted to nylon shirts, hence IED = 0. As income increases in phase B the consumer enters the market for cotton shirts and IED = > 1. Eventually the consumer's demand for cotton shirts is satisfied and in phase C further increases in income do not lead to any further increase in demand, hence IED = 0. Eventually at very high incomes the consumer enters the market for silk shirts and the demand for cotton shirts declines as income rises hence IED = negative. (< 1).

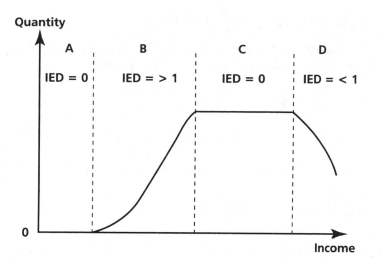

Figure 7.11

11 Cross elasticity of demand

Cross elasticity of demand measures the **responsiveness in the quantity demanded of one good to the change in the price of another good.** Where goods are close substitutes or complements cross elasticity is high. It is measured as:

$$\text{Cross elasticity of demand for X with respect to Y} = \frac{\text{Percentage change in quantity demanded of good X}}{\text{Percentage change in the price of good Y}}$$

If the two goods are close substitutes then an increase (+) in the price of good Y will result in a transfer of demand to good X, (+) thus

$$\text{Exy} = \frac{+}{+} = +$$

and cross elasticity of demand is positive.

Alternatively if the two goods are consumed together, i.e. are complements, then an increase (+) in the price of good Y will reduce the demand for both goods (-) thus

$$\text{Exy} = \frac{-}{+} = -$$

and the cross elasticity of demand is therefore **negative**. If there is no relationship between the two goods then

$$\text{Exy} = 0$$

A practical example of cross elasticity resulted from the doubling of coffee prices in 1975 which followed the failure of the Brazilian coffee harvest due to frost and caused a transfer of demand to the closest substitute, tea, the price of which rose shortly afterwards as a consequence. Astute commodity buyers aware of the nature of cross elasticity entered the tea market shortly after the rise in coffee prices.

12 Elasticity of supply

The concept of elasticity also refers to **supply** and **elasticity of supply** can be defined as the **responsiveness of the quantity supplied to changes in price**.

$$\text{The formula for Es} = \frac{\text{\%age or proportionate change in QS}}{\text{\%age or proportionate change in price}}$$

Figure 7.12 illustrates different supply elasticities. It should be noted that any straight line supply curve passing through the origin is unitary. Elasticity of supply = 0 occurs when supply is fixed and cannot be increased, for example Rembrandt paintings.

13 Elasticity of supply and time

The time period involved is very important when discussing elasticity of supply. There are three time periods which are relevant to elasticity of supply; the momentary, the short run and the long run.

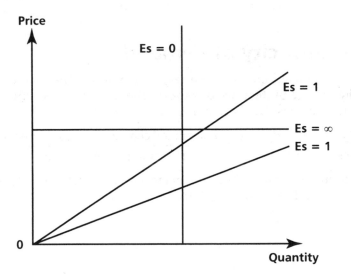

Figure 7.12

The momentary period is the period in which **no adjustments** of either fixed or variable factors of production can occur in response to a change in demand.

The short run is that period in which **variable factors** only can adjust to a new situation.

The **long run** is that period in which both **fixed** and **variable factors** can adjust.

In Figure 7.13(a) there is an increase in demand from D to D', but in the momentary period supplies are fixed at Q and supply is completely inelastic. For example, if demand for fresh fruit suddenly increases supplies at a fruit market cannot be immediately increased. After a period of time has passed supplies can however be increased as variable factors are used more intensively; in the example fruit farmers work longer hours and send more to market. As a result supply becomes more elastic, i.e. S' in 7.13(b), and the price falls to P², In the long run both fixed and variable factors have had time to adjust, fruit farmers will have increased their acreage, employed more labour and machines, and new farmers will have entered the industry. Supply has become more elastic, S^2 in Figure 7.13(c) with the long run price P^3 lower than P^2, with higher demand at Q^3. Whether the long run price P^3 is above or below the original price P depends upon how easily the industry has been able to obtain the additional factors of production it requires for expansion or whether the required factors had to be attracted from alternative uses by paying more for them. Also the extent to which the industry was able to gain economies of scale (see Chapter 13) from its expansion will affect the long run equilibrium price.

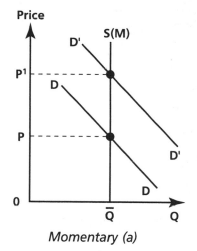

Momentary (a)

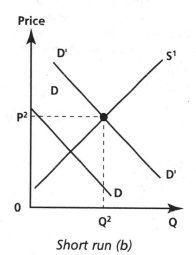

Short run (b)

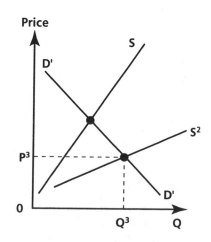

Long run (c)

Figure 7.13a, b, and c

Self assessment questions

1 Why is the gradient of the demand curve not a reliable indicator of price elasticity of demand?

2 With reference to Table 7.1 calculate the price elasticity of demand for a price increase

   (i) from 2p to 3p
   (ii) from 5p to 6p.

3 State the three limiting cases where the demand curve is a guide to elasticity of demand.

4 What are the three time periods relevant to Elasticity of Supply?

5 What factors determine the price elasticity of demand for commodity?

6 **(a)** Define each of the following terms:
   - price elasticity of demand
   - income elasticity of demand
   - cross elasticity of demand.

   Describe briefly the factors that determine each of them.

   (b) Below is the demand schedule for a product.

Price (£ per unit)	Demand (units per week)
10	400
9	500
8	600
7	700
6	800
5	900
4	1000
3	1100

Calculate the price elasticity of demand and comment on your results when
(a) the price is reduced from £9 to £8 per unit.
(b) the price is reduced from £5 to £4 per unit

8

Market analysis

1 Dynamic and static analysis

Incorporating demand and supply elasticities with the previous analysis of the determinants of market price makes possible the study of **dynamic models** of market adjustment, rather than the **static** analysis undertaken so far which simply describes the movement from one price to another. Dynamic analysis becomes necessary when the response of supply to changes in market price is characterised by considerable time lags, for example in agriculture where the **decision** to increase output is taken well in advance of any actual increase in output due to the time required for the crop to grow. One such simple dynamic model is known as the **cobweb theorem**.

2 The cobweb theorem

The cobweb theorem is best illustrated by the example of agricultural markets, particularly those where the actions of producers are uncoordinated with no central control and where no co-operatives exist. Such markets are characterised by substantial and frequent fluctuations in both price and output. The principle can be illustrated by referring to the production of coffee in South America. Given the correct climatic conditions, soil and altitude, coffee is a highly prolific crop and is certainly the easiest crop for the poor peasant farmers to grow, but with a time lag of between 3–5 years between the planting of the coffee tree and it bearing fruit. If in any particular year the price of coffee is high and growers receive a good return they will respond by increasing their acreage, of course they all respond in the same way with the consequence being that in the following period supply exceeds demand and the price falls. The response to the reduction in price may result in reduced plantings and shortages in the following period, hence there are alternating shortages and surpluses with corresponding fluctuations in price. An alternative response to the price fall following increased acreage may be that the individual farmer, unaware that the other farmers are doing exactly the same thing, actually increases his acreage in the face of a lower price in order to try to maintain his real income by increasing output, but because they all respond in the same uncoordinated way surpluses become ever larger and prices and therefore farm incomes continually decline. This is the situation in which Brazil's farmers found themselves in the period up to the 1970s. The same market characteristics however apply to most agricultural commodities, for example grain, sugar beet, potatoes etc. These price fluctuations may cause severe problems for the developing nations where incomes are dependent upon a narrow range of primary products.

3 The converging/stable cobweb

According to the cobweb theorem, therefore, the supply of a commodity in the current period depends upon the **price (P) which prevailed in the previous period (P_{t-1}) where-as the quantity demanded depends upon the price in the current period (P_t).**
Supply can therefore be represented as

$$St = f (P_{t-1})$$

and demand as

$$Dt = f (P_t)$$

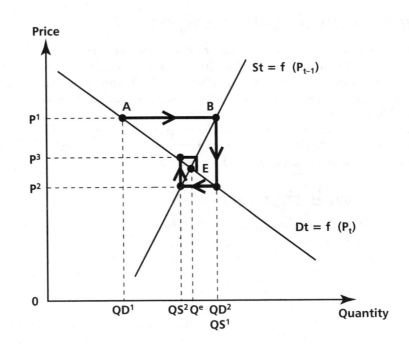

Figure 8.1

In Figure 8.1 the original price prevailing on the market is P^1 and growers respond to this price by ensuring that supply will be QS^1 or B, in the following period by appropriate planting. When this supply arrives on the market in the current year at the price prevailing in the previous period, P^1, only QD^1 will be demanded, which creates a surplus in the market of QD^1–QS^1 (or A–B). Because farmers must clear their existing stocks supply in this period QS^1 is totally inelastic consequently the surplus will drive the price down until there is sufficient demand to clear current stocks. Price therefore falls to P^2 where existing stocks are cleared. The price P^2 is now the price prevailing for the following year for which the appropriate supply is QS^2. At price P^2 however, demand is QD^2 resulting in a shortage of QD^2–QS^2. This shortage will push the market price up to P^3 which will clear the market. A similar sequence of events follows but with **successive surpluses and shortages becoming smaller and smaller until the market converges upon the long run equilibrium price at E**. The converging cobweb occurs when the supply curve is less elastic than the demand curve.

4 The diverging/unstable cobweb

The alternative model is the **diverging cobweb** where the market situation is **unstable** and departs further and further from equilibrium over successive periods. Such a situation occurs when the elasticity of supply is greater than the elasticity of demand. The diverging cobweb model is illustrated in Figure 8.2.

Analysis of the divergent cobweb model is identical to the convergent cobweb, however in this case the quantity supplied changes to a greater extent than the quantity demanded in response to any change in price. As a consequence **the market moves away from equilibrium over successive periods as surpluses and shortages become progressively larger**, the market is therefore unstable.

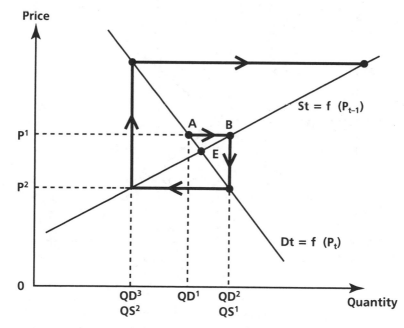

Figure 8.2

5 Buffer stocks

Because of the problems created by the large fluctuations in agricultural output and incomes, governments have introduced various agricultural stabilisation policies in the attempt to stabilise farm incomes and output. One policy which has been used in various countries is a **buffer stock** scheme. These schemes attempt to maintain farm incomes by means of a guaranteed or target price, which is maintained by means of a government agency which purchases surplus stocks and stores them, reselling them later during periods of shortage.

In Figure 8.3 if the **target price** is set at the average free market price Pe and in one particular year actual output is Q^2 the surplus Qe – Q^2 is withdrawn from the market by the, government agency which enters the market as a buyer in order to maintain the target price of Pe, this surplus is then added to the buffer stocks in government warehouses. In the following year if actual output is Q^1 then the shortage, Q^1–Qe is eliminated by releasing stock from the government warehouses forcing the price down from P^1 to the target price Pe. Schemes such as this however rarely work smoothly, for instance there is no reason why shortages should automatically follow surpluses, and there may be successive periods of surplus to be added to stocks with no opportunity for disposal Also the costs of storage may be considerable with interest charges, deterioration and refrigeration for meat and butter. Problems also arise with the setting of the target price, because of either the difficulty of forecasting the average market price, or as the result of desire to boost farm income or encourage greater output, the target price may be set above the equilibrium price, for example at P^1 in Figure 8.3.

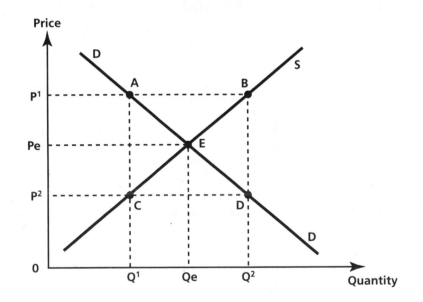

Figure 8.3

As a consequence farmers will be encouraged to increase output to Q^2 and the surplus of Qe–Q^2 will have to be purchased and added to official stocks in every period. The knowledge that the minimum price is guaranteed and all production can be sold will encourage producers to produce excess output. The continuous additions to stock can become a financial problem for the government, but also the existence of vast food stocks being unused may become a source of political embarrassment for the authorities. The financing of the stocks also becomes an issue, if they are financed from general taxation then the incomes of the farming community are being subsidised by the non-farming community hence a non-voluntary transfer of income occurs. **The Common Agricultural Policy (CAP)** of the EU is an example of such a scheme. The high intervention (target) prices have resulted in the butter and beef 'mountains' and the wine 'lake' causing acute embarrassment to the EU Commission. In order to off load the surplus stocks they were sold off outside the EU at a price below the target price. This dumping of surplus stocks at prices below the target price constitutes a transfer of income from taxpayers in the EU to consumers outside it.

6 Price stabilisation

Schemes of the type outlined above stabilise prices at the target price but do not necessarily stabilise farm incomes. Total farm incomes are given by the target price (Pe) × output (Q) i.e. Pe × Q When output is Q^2 total farm incomes are Pe × Q^2 and when output is Q^1 incomes are Pe × Q^1, and Pe × Q^2>Pe × Q^1 .What in fact happens is that farm incomes vary in the same direction as outputs so when output is large incomes are large and vice versa. If the objective is to stabilise farm incomes then the demand curve for output will need to be unitary (=1) and the target price should be allowed to vary in proportion to output. As a consequence if output increases by 10% then price is allowed to fall by 10% and vice versa, which, given the unitary demand curve, maintains an unchanged income for farmers. Therefore, where the authorities wish to stabilise incomes they will seek to influence the demand side of the market but will need to be prepared to adjust target prices accordingly.

7 Buffer stocks in practice

Buffer stock schemes have generally met with the type of problems outlined above, for example in the attempt to maintain coffee prices the Brazilian government's intervention scheme resulted in having sufficient stocks in official warehouses to meet total world demand for several years, until the 1975 crop was depleted by frost. In the same year the crop of the world's second largest producer Angola was ruined by civil war. As a result of this combination of events the world price of coffee rose by almost 300% over the next two years. As a result of the higher world price for coffee, as the cobweb theory predicts, coffee planting increased substantially and by 1980 the real price of coffee had returned to the 1975 level as output increased.

8 Alternative approaches

There are various **alternative approaches to maintaining or raising prices and incomes** which may be used either independently or together with buffer stock schemes.

- **Quotas** on the production of a commodity whereby each producer is given a limit to the amount which can be produced.
- **Financial incentives to diversify** into alternative crops, for example the payment of a bonus to the farmer for every coffee tree replaced with cotton.
- **Export quota schemes** whereby each producer country is given a quota as to how much of a commodity they can export, for example the International Coffee Agreement (ICA), no longer in operation, which restricted the export of coffee.
- **Producer cartels** which are agreements between producer countries to withhold supplies from the world market in order to keep prices higher and thereby increase their revenues. This was done very successfully by the Organisation of Petroleum Exporting Countries (OPEC) in 1973/74 and 1979/80. It is difficult to maintain such cartels in the long run however because eventually it serves the interests of at least one member to

leave the cartel and undercut the other members; seldom is a cartel in the interests of all members at all times. Also the higher prices will eventually have some affect on demand which declines, for example in the case of high oil prices by economising on oil consumption and the development of alternative energy sources, which together with the reduction in demand resulting from the slow down in economic activity made it difficult for the OPEC cartel to continue to dominate world oil prices.

Self assessment questions

1 Distinguish between dynamic and static market analysis.

2 What is meant by:
   (a) Diverging cobweb price behaviour.
   (b) Converging cobweb price behaviour.

3 How do agricultural buffer stock schemes operate?

4 Why do cartels tend to break down eventually?

9

The firm's costs

1 The importance of costs

During the act of production the firm will incur certain costs and it is necessary to examine how these costs behave as output changes. It is necessary to consider how costs behave with a fixed set of plant and capacity, and also how they behave over the longer period when plant and capacity can be varied.

2 Costs

Costs can be classified as either **fixed costs** or **variable costs**.

Fixed costs (sometimes referred to as overhead costs) do not vary with output, they remain constant, or fixed. Examples of fixed costs (FC) include rent, rates, interest on loans, depreciation of plant and equipment. No matter to what extent the firm is utilising its capacity this group of costs remains unchanged. This should not be taken to mean that FCs never change, for example, rates may increase; but they do remain constant over fairly long periods, and more importantly, do not vary with output .
   Variable costs (VC) are costs which vary directly with output. Examples of variable costs (also referred to as direct costs) may include wages, raw materials and power. When output is zero variable cost will be zero and they rise directly with output.
   Total costs (TC) are the sum of fixed and variable costs, i.e.

$$TC = FC + VC$$

When output is zero TC = FC and as output rises TC increases with the increase in VC. Fixed, variable and total costs are illustrated in Figure 9. 1.

3 Average costs

In order to analyse the effect of output on costs however, it is necessary to identify costs more closely with units of production, i.e. the cost per unit. Total costs need to be converted into **average costs**. To achieve this all that is required is to divide FC, VC and TC by output (Q). Hence we obtain **average fixed cost (AFC)**, **average variable cost (AVC)** and **average total cost (AC)**.

i.e.

$$AFC = \frac{FC}{Q}$$

$$AVC = \frac{VC}{Q}$$

$$AC = \frac{TC}{Q}$$

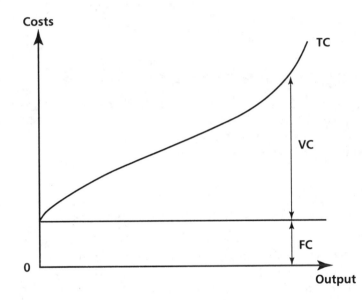

Figure 9.1

Figure 9.2 represents these average costs diagramatically. Because FC is constant but spread over an increasing number of units it falls over its entire length. AVC falls then rises slowly, whilst AC falls then rises in a U-shaped curve.

Mathematically AC = AFC + AVC.

4 The AC curve

The AC is typically a U-shaped curve, with average costs of production falling and then rising. The AC curve falls initially for the following reasons:

As fixed costs are spread over more units of production the average fixed cost per unit will fall, i.e. fixed costs are £50 and we produce 50 units, each unit carries £1 of fixed cost, if output rises to 100 units each unit carries only 50p and so on.

As more variable factors are added to the fixed factors (land and capital) there will be increasing returns, eventually however diminishing returns will set in, causing costs to rise again. After reaching a minimum the AC curve begins to rise because:

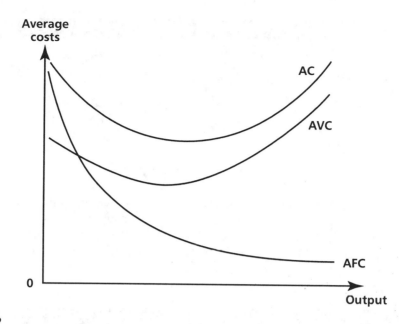

Figure 9.2

- As output increases we may have to employ less efficient labour, as we can assume that the 'best' labour will have been employed first.
- Less efficient machinery may be utilised which would not be used at lower outputs.
- Labour may have to work overtime at higher hourly wage rates.
- Machinery worked consistently at full capacity is liable to more frequent breakdowns.
- The managerial problems of co-ordination and control become greater at higher outputs.

The optimum (or ideal) output for the firm is where AC is at minimum, at the lowest point on the AC curve.

5 Normal profit

A further essential point about average cost is that in economics cost includes **normal profit.** Normal profit is that rate of return which is just sufficient to keep the factors of production in their current use and prevent them transferring to any alternative. It can therefore be considered as the cost to the entrepreneur of keeping the factors of production in their current use.

6 Marginal cost

Marginal cost is another very important concept in the study of the firm's costs. Whenever the term 'marginal' is used in economics it refers to the extra, or incremental unit. In the case of costs marginal cost refers to the **addition to total costs incurred by producing one extra unit of output.**

Table 9.1				
Q	FC	VC	TC	MC
0	30	0	30	
				15
1	30	15	45	
				10
2	30	25	55	

7 The interaction of AC and MC

Table 9.1 illustrates the concept of marginal cost where it is shown against the mid-points of the increase in output (Q) because it is the increase in costs incurred by increasing output by 1 extra unit. As FC is constant MC is the same as the increase in VC.

The derivation of the columns in Table 9.2 is straightforward and is explained in 2 and 3. The average and marginal cost data is plotted in Figure 9.3.

Table 9.2					
Q	FC	VC	TC	AC	MC
0	30	0	30		
					15
1	30	15	45	45	
					10
2	30	25	55	27½	
					5
3	30	30	60	20	
					10
4	30	40	70	17½	
					30
5	30	70	100	20	
					50
6	30	120	150	25	
					95
7	30	215	245	35	

It can be seen that the MC curve falls then rises rapidly **cutting the AC curve at its lowest point**. Whenever MC is below AC, AC is falling and whenever MC is above AC, AC is rising, MC **always** cutting AC at its lowest point. This must be the case because of the relationship between MC and AC.

This can be explained by analogy with a darts contest. If a player had scored an average of 100 in ten games and then in his eleventh game scored only 90 then his average would fall to 99. If on the other hand he had scored 110 his average would have risen to 101. It is therefore the additional, or marginal, game which determines the average, and if the marginal score is below the average the average falls, and if the marginal score is above the average, the average rises.

It can be clearly seen from Figure 9.3 that the lowest per unit cost, or optimal output, is at the lowest point on the AC curve, which coincides with the point where MC crosses AC.

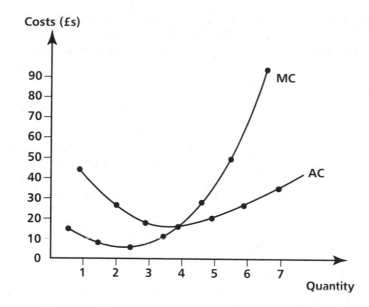

Figure 9.3

8 Short run and long run costs

All the costs mentioned so far assume that the firm has fixed plant and equipment, i.e. the firm is in a **short-run situation**. It is quite possible however, and indeed probable, that the firm will vary its plant over the longer period, particularly if it suffers rising costs from a given plant size it may well expand its capacity.

As the firm encounters rising costs it may decide to re-invest and expand its capacity. This new set of plant will have an entirely new AC curve with its optimal output higher than for the previous plant. This is referred to as changing the **scale** of production and it is necessary to consider the effect of such changes on **costs**, i.e. the behaviour of **long-run costs**.

Figure 9.4 illustrates the effects of changes in the scale of production on long run costs. The firm's first set of plant has short run average cost curve SRAC^1, but eventually costs rise so the firm invests in a new set of plant which has a greater capacity, with cost curve SRAC^2, this is repeated for scales 3 and 4, which may represent an overall period of 20 years or

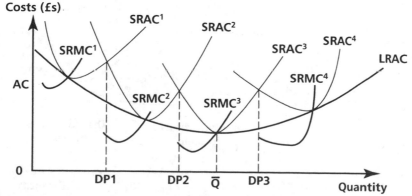

Figure 9.4

longer. Note that when the new plant is introduced, i.e. decision points 1, 2 and 3 its costs may be higher than the minimum point on the old plant, this is because its capacity may not be fully utilised initially, but as output grows it moves down its AC to the lowest point.

9 Economies of scale

It should also be noted in Figure 9.4 that the minimum point of AC for each successive plant size is lower up to $\bar{Q}$ and then begins to rise again. This is because the **economies of scale** resulting from large scale production tend to reduce costs whilst after $\bar{Q}$ **diseconomies of scale** set in and costs start to rise again. $\bar{Q}$ is the optimal long run combination of plant and output but firms rarely recognise when they are at such a point and will more frequently have to attempt to move back to it, after encountering rising costs, by a process of rationalisation.

10 Long run average cost

By drawing a smooth curve which is tangential to each short run AC curve we can derive the **long run average cost curve (LRAC)**, sometimes referred to as the long run '**planning envelope**'. The lowest point on this LRAC curve is the long run optimal output $\bar{Q}$. This coincides with the lowest point on SRAC[3].

The long run average cost curve (LRAC) shown in Figure 9.4 may have to be modified in reality as it may not have the smooth U-shape described. This is because the economies of scale usually apply with some degree of certainty as the firm expands its capacity, however the diseconomies of scale are more imprecise and may be offset by skilful management until late in the growth of the firm. As a consequence the shape of the LRAC may be more like that illustrated in Figure 9.5. Up to output Q costs fall as scale increases but beyond Q there is a substantial range of operations where costs remain unchanged and there are constant returns to scale. Diseconomies of scale only become established as capacity expands beyond Q', and the actual point at which Q' occurs will vary widely between different firms and industries. It is therefore possible in some circumstances for firms to expand their capacity over a large range without encountering rising costs. However, at some point they will almost certainly encounter rising long run costs as diseconomies of scale set in.

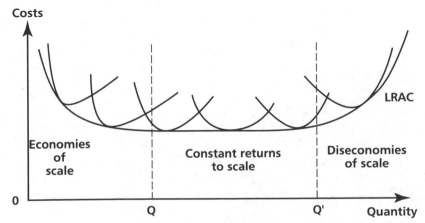

Figure 9.5

11 Internal economies of scale

Internal economies of scale are benefits to the firm which are generated internally and result from larger scale production. They have the effect of reducing the per unit (AC) costs of production. Such economies result from:

Purchasing economies: Larger firms buy their raw materials and other requirements in larger quantities and in return receive larger discounts from suppliers which contribute to cost reduction. Smaller firms are not able to take advantage of such discounts and therefore pay more for their materials.

Marketing economies: Larger firms are able to make more effective use of their salesforce. A salesman can negotiate an order for 500 units in almost the same amount of time as one for 100 units. Administrative costs also do not rise in proportion with order size and cost per item ordered are generally much lower. Larger firms are also able to utilise more effective advertising media such as television, and where the product range is wide the advertising of the brand name helps to sell all the firm's products.

Managerial economies: Large firms can afford, and justify, the employment of specialist managers such as accountants, production managers, sales managers, lawyers etc., whereas in the small firm the managers may have to manage all aspects of the business. The greater degree of specialisation in management leads to greater efficiency.

Financial economies: Large firms are generally able to raise capital more easily and cheaply than small firms. They have more substantial assets and with a sound trading record, financial institutions see them as representing a lower degree of risk, since they can lay claim to those assets if the firm defaults on payments on a loan.

Technical economies: Larger firms have greater scope for the division of labour, and specialisation can be carried to a higher degree. This facilitates the introduction of more machinery and specialised equipment which raises productivity. As output increases labour costs per unit of output tend to decline.

Indivisibility: Many production processes are either technically impossible, or not financially viable, on a small scale – they are indivisible in that they cannot be broken down into small scale production. Many chemicals can only be produced commercially on a large scale, the same is true of steel and cars. As firms become larger they are able to take advantage of these more efficient, large scale, manufacturing processes.

Risk-bearing economies: Larger organisations tend to produce a more diverse range of products; this creates a form of protection in that if one product fails the firm has others which will enable it to survive. Large firms can also afford to undertake high risk activities such as research and development into new products. High costs will be incurred during the development stage without any certainty of making an adequate return. When such activity is successful, however, it can be highly profitable, for example the drug industry's expenditure on research is vast but so too are the profits made on a successful new product.

The principle of multiples: this is a further economy favouring large companies. Machines tend to have different operating speeds and it can be difficult to link them 'end-on' in a production process. This is particularly difficult with only a few machines as it becomes very difficult to ensure a balanced flow which ensures that each machine is being fully utilised. With more machines however, larger firms find it easier to organise them in linked processes which ensures that they are all fully utilised.

12 Diseconomies of scale

Diseconomies of scale will set in at some stage in the growth of the firm and result in rising per unit costs. These are more difficult to identify but tend to be more managerial in nature:

- As the firm grows the problems of **co-ordination and control** tend to grow rapidly after a certain point and the costs of employing more management (which is not directly productive) grows disproportionately .
- Problems of **communication** arise, both lateral and vertical communications become difficult, not only is it difficult to ensure that instructions are received, but also that they are carried out correctly.
- As organisations grow they may involve production at several separate plants, and the **co-ordination** of activities become less effective.
- Large organisations tend to become more **impersonal**, there is no feeling of 'belonging', hence attitudes of apathy tend to develop, and at worst the workforce becomes 'demotivated' or 'alienated'.

13 External economies of scale

The economies of scale discussed above are all **internal**, they are generated from within the firm as a consequence of its growth. Another group of economies referred to as **external economies of scale** are generated not as a result of the growth of the firm, but as a consequence of the concentration and growth of an industry within an area. Briefly the major external economies of scale are as a result of:

- A pool of labour with appropriate skills within the area.
- Shared research facilities.
- Appropriate financial facilities.
- The growth of component and other suppliers within the area.
- Appropriate educational courses at colleges and universities
- An appropriate infrastructure developing, i.e. roads, harbours and transport.

These factors tend to reduce the operating costs of all the firms in the industry.

14 Avoiding diseconomies of scale

The existence of large firms that do not exhibit dis-economies of scale suggests that they are not necessarily inevitable. The Toyota motor car company is now a vast multi-national manufacturer which despite its size seems to be enjoying ever reducing costs. An insight into how this is achieved through the adoption of 'lean production' techniques is described in detail in 'The Machine That Changed The World' (Womack, Jones and Roos, *Rawson* 1990). Some of the ways in which dis-economies appear to be off-set include:

- Modern computerised management control techniques such as manufacturing resource planning (MRP 11) may overcome some of the problems of co-ordination and control in large plants.
- Communication and control have been improved by modern flatter management structures in place of the old hierarchical structures.
- Prevailing management methods which involve employee participation or

empowerment which in turn involves giving people working in teams some control over their own decisions and immediate work activities. Some of the problems of decision making and demotivation are overcome in this way.

- Making greater use of suppliers who have assemblies or sub-assemblies sub-contracted to them. These 'first tier' suppliers then co-ordinate all the activities further down the supply chain. For example Toyota deals only with the supplier of seats and the seat supplier is responsible for the co-ordination of the supply of seat components, the assembly of seats to a given specification, and they deliver to the Toyota factory. In effect Toyota take advantages of their suppliers' skills and economies and build them into their own.
- The introduction of cost centres or small business units within the larger organisation so, for example, one product line becomes treated as a business unit responsible for its own costs, operations and profitability within the overall organisational structure.
- Strategies such as Just-in-Time (JIT) stock management and Total Quality Management (TQM) which have as their objectives the elimination of investment in stocks and the elimination of waste throughout the organisation. These 'lean' production methods give much tighter, more responsive, control over manufacturing operations with subsequent improvements in quality and reductions in operating costs.
- 'Outsourcing' non-core activities. These are activities which add nothing to the value of the product and should therefore be undertaken by an outside contractor who has a 'distinctive competence' in this specific area. For example a manufacturer may contract-out canteen provision to a specialist caterer.
- New technology provides opportunities for overcoming the tendency for costs to rise.

It may be that many firms have long run average cost curves that are quite flat at the bottom rather than the U-shape assumed above, giving constant returns over quite wide ranges of output. The question which must be asked however is can any firm enjoy permanently falling costs? The answer must be that they cannot or costs would fall eventually to zero which is illogical, hence it is really a question of where the firm actually is on its long-run cost curve.

Self assessment questions

1 Distinguish between fixed costs and variable costs.

2 Why do average costs fall and then rise?

3 At what point does the marginal cost curve intersect the average cost curve?

4 In what sense is normal profit a cost?

5 What is meant by internal economies of scale?

6 Explain the term diseconomies of scale.

7 What is meant by external economies of scale, and why do they occur?

8 How is the firm's long run average cost curve derived?

9 Why does the long run average cost curve initially fall and then rise?

10 Under what circumstances may a firm achieve constant returns to scale?

10

The growth of the business unit

1 Motives for growth

There appears to be an inevitable tendency for successful organisations to grow in size. The effect on the firm's costs will be one very important motive for growth, but there are other motives, and in this chapter we analyse what these various motives may be, and the form and direction that this growth may take.

The most frequent motives for growth can be identified as:

- To **gain the economies of scale** (see Chapter 9).
- To **gain dominance over the market** by gaining a larger market share, i.e. the monopoly motive.
- To **diversify into a wider range of products** in order to gain greater security, e.g. Imperial Tobacco now produce over 60 different products, as diverse as crisps, cigarettes and cardboard cartons.

2 Methods of growth

Firms may grow by either internal expansion or externally by merging with, or acquiring, other firms.

Internal expansion is most likely to occur in an industry which is relatively new and the market is still growing. Growth of this type usually takes the form of expanding the existing amount of plant and manufacturing units. The increase in capacity will enable the firm to:

- Increase the output of its existing products.
- Enter new markets with its existing products.
- Produce a wider range of products.

External growth refers to growth by means of either **merger** or **acquisition**.
Growth by **merger** occurs when two, usually similarly sized firms, decide to join together and merge their separate identities into one.

Growth by **acquisition** occurs when a business grows by taking over the plants or markets of an existing firm, sometimes referred to as a 'take-over'.

External growth by such methods may make use of a **holding company**. A holding company is formed specifically for the purpose of gaining a controlling interest (51% of the shares) in a number of other companies. The companies taken over may remain as separate units, but the main policy decisions will be made centrally by the holding company. Examples of holding companies include the Trafalgar House Group whose interests include insurance and shipbuilding, the Imperial Tobacco Company mentioned above and Sears (Holdings) Ltd. which has interests in activities as diverse as shipbuilding, footwear, engineering and retailing, and the British American Tobacco Co. whose interests include tobacco and insurance (Eagle Star Insurance). 1986 was a year of almost unprecedented merger activity with many large groups either merging or taking over other groups. The motive for these mergers was either to strengthen the firms market position in the face of the difficult trading conditions or to diversify into new product areas, generally for the same reason. Mergers included Habitat and British Homestores, Argyll and Distillers, and Amstrad and Sinclair. 1995 saw another record year with £66 billion of assets changing hands, the most significant being the takeover of Wellcome by Glaxo which created a drug company which now dominates the market.

3 Integration

Growth by acquisition or merger is also referred to as **integration**. Integration is normally classified according to the direction of the integration, which may be:

Horizontal:
The merging of two firms at the same stage of production.

Vertical:
- **backwards** towards sources of raw materials.
- **forwards** towards the final market.

4 Horizontal integration

Horizontal integration occurs when firms **engaged in the same stage of production** come under a single control. This is very common at the retail stage, for example the merger of Boots and Timothy Whites, and that between Habitat and Mothercare. Some of the UK's largest companies have been formed as a result of such mergers including: United Biscuits, Associated Biscuits, Associated Foods, British Leyland, and GEC. An illustration of a horizontal integration would be the merger of two woollen textile manufacturers. Horizontal mergers may occur in order to gain some of the economies of scale mentioned in Chapter 9. In particular the following economies may be gained:

- The establishment of a central purchasing department buying the combined requirements of all the companies in the group will gain better discounts for the bulk buying of components and raw materials. Centralised purchasing also facilitates the establishment of better buying and stock control systems, and can employ the expertise of specialist buyers. Large organisations pay considerably less for their supplies than do smaller companies. This is particularly important in retailing where these purchasing economies give a significant advantage to the large retail group over the small independent.

- Financial economies – see Chapter 9.
- Marketing economies – see Chapter 9.
- Technical economies – in addition to the points mentioned in Chapter 9, horizontal integration may create savings in research and development effort. Instead of competing and thereby reproducing costly research effort, research can be centralised, and the pooling of facilities, expertise and effort, can bring considerable savings. Also the combined output of the merged firms may justify the use of larger more efficient machines which would not be fully utilised by the output of a single firm. The same argument can be applied to new technology where robotic production systems and sophisticated computerised control systems can only be justified on the basis of large outputs.
- Managerial economies – see Chapter 9. Larger firms can afford to employ specialised management, and as there is more scope for division of labour the degree of managerial specialisation can be carried further than in small firms, with the subsequent benefits. Also larger firms can afford to pay the high salaries necessary to attract the most talented managers.
- The merger in 1986 between the rival electronics firms Amstrad and Sinclair provides an interesting example of a horizontal merger where the technical expertise and inventiveness of the Sinclair company was combined with the marketing expertise of Amstrad, to the mutual advantage of both groups.
- Some significant examples of horizontal integration in manufacturing industry have been: Allied Breweries and Showerings, GEC and English Electric, British Motor Holdings and Leyland, and the takeover of Jaguar by the Ford Motor Company.

5 Vertical integration

Vertical integration refers to mergers which take place between firms who are engaged in different stages of a production process. Forward vertical integration occurs when a firm merges with a firm at a later stage in the manufacturing process, for example a clothing manufacturer acquiring a chain of retail outlets. Backward vertical integration occurs when the merger takes place with a firm at an earlier stage in the manufacturing process, for example a woollen textile firm acquiring a weaving firm. When the entire manufacturing process from raw materials to distribution of the finished goods are under the control of a single firm the firm is referred to as 'fully integrated'. At the other extreme where all components are bought out and merely assembled by the firm, the firm is said to be 'disintegrated'. Ford of America was an example of a fully integrated firm. Growth by vertical integration has in the past been a characteristic of the motor car industry as motor car manufacturers attempted to gain control of component suppliers. Forward vertical integration in the motor car industry mainly occurs in the form of manufacturers attempting to establish distribution and dealership networks. In the brewing industry it is usually in the form of breweries taking over public houses. In fact the majority of vertical forward integrations are of this type, with manufacturing firms attempting to ensure retail outlets for their products.

6 The merits of vertical integration

Vertical integration may well achieve many of the internal economies of scale mentioned in Chapter 9. There may however be additional advantages to be gained.

Backward integration may be motivated by the desire to ensure the supply of materials which are relatively scarce. This is essentially a defensive motive but it may also be aggressive if these supplies are then denied to competitors.

Many modern manufacturing processes have very stringent quality control requirements for their components, and attempt to run their production on minimal stocks, they therefore have very tight delivery schedules for supplies. Vertical integration by acquiring component suppliers ensures closer control over the quality of supplies and their conformance with specifications, and also guarantees deliveries. The assurance of quality requirements brings savings in the form of lower inspection costs and lower reject rates during production. Guaranteed delivery performance by suppliers allows firms to reduce their stock levels of components and production materials which reduces their inventory carrying costs; which can be a considerable expense. Many large manufacturers favour such integration as it enables them, with the aid of micro-technology, to introduce techniques such as materials requirements planning, by which supplies are matched exactly with production requirements, resulting in considerable savings in stockholding costs. Such integration has been greatly favoured by the Japanese car and electrical industries.

The 'end-on' linking of processes is also facilitated by vertical integration, and if this is followed by the concentration of production into a single plant then there may be considerable technical economies. The integration of machines enables machine timings to be set in such a way as to avoid excess stocks of work-in-progress building up, or machines standing idle waiting for another slower part of the process to catch up. Modern steel works provide a good example of integrated production where the production of iron and steel, and the rolling of steel are combined in one continuous process.

Control over distribution networks is also a source of cost saving. Not only are outlets assured for the firm's products and the costs of distribution reduced, but the firm is also more able to match its production levels to current market demand, particularly where ownership extends to the retail level and market information can be readily fed back to the plant level where sales forecasts and production schedules can be updated in the light of the latest information. This avoids the holding of excess stocks of finished goods or lost sales as a result of shortages. Ownership of distribution channels and retail outlets also enables the firm to eliminate the wholesale function reducing costs and increasing profitability and, also assisting in the marketing and promoting of the product.

Product diversification may also result from vertical integration. This is the widening of the firm's product range and is a form of protection against the possibility of the failure of a single product putting at risk the survival of the firm. It is in fact one of the economies of scale; that of risk bearing. One example is the aquisition by BMW of Rover, the producer of the Land Rover, in order to gain access to the four-wheel drive market.

Tube Investments' acquisition of The British Aluminium Company who produced lightweight tubing, is an example of backward vertical integration, and the acquisition, also by Tube Investments, of Raleigh Industries is an example of forward vertical integration. Tube Investments then possessed a tube manufacturer and also a firm which utilised tubing in the manufacture of lightweight bicycles.

7 Recent trends

The majority of mergers in recent years have been of the horizontal type. These have been mainly defensive in character in order to consolidate market shares in the face of world recession and growing international competition. Despite this the opportunities to gain economies of scale remain one of the main motives for both types of merger, but are still only a single element in a complex decision.

Table 10.1	1965–73	1978	1982	1987	1994
Horizontal (%)	78	53	65	67	88
Vertical (%)	5	13	5	3	5
Conglomerate	17	34	30	30	7

8 Conglomerate mergers

Conglomerate mergers are mergers which are not strictly lateral or vertical but are between companies producing a product (or range of products) which are not directly related. The **objective** may be to reduce risk by diversifying or to enter a new market when the existing market offers little hope for further growth. They are frequently associated with **multi national companies** and **holding companies**. Examples are the Imperial Tobacco Group and Sears (Holdings) Ltd., mentioned earlier, and British American Tobacco which acquired Eagle Star Insurance, and Hanson Trust's acquisition of the London Brick Co. and in 1986 the Imperial Tobacco and United Biscuits Groups.

The year 1987/88 saw a very high level of mergers and acquisitions in the UK by industrial and commercial companies, however a second take-over boom emerged in 1995/96 with acquisitions reaching a record £67.7 billion. Internationally one of the most significant mergers was within the United States aircraft industry with the acquisition of McDonnell Douglas by Boeing which will give the combined company dominance over civilian and military aircraft production, including helicopters, and posed a severe threat to the European Airbus project.

Conglomerate mergers are currently less fashionable however, as the trend is for organisations to focus on their 'core activities,' due to the problems they have experienced in the management of diversified business activities. For example Hanson is breaking up into four separate business units, and recently Unilever sold its interest in chemicals and food flavourings to ICI.

9 Small firms

Despite the fact that economies of scale appear to offer substantial benefits to large firms many industries are still characterised by the survival of small firms. It is necessary to consider therefore why small firms survive and why they are so prevalent in some industries, and also why in some industries both large and small firms exist alongside each other. The main reasons are outlined below.

Where personal attention is involved and growth of the firm would involve loss of personal attention to detail. Examples are hairdressing and bespoke tailoring.

Where the total market is small, output will not be sufficient to achieve the necessary levels of specialisation and division of labour. Examples include retailing in isolated communities where only 'general' shops can survive because the limited demand prohibits specialised retailing. Garages tend to be small because the market is limited by the distance people are willing to travel for car repairs, and also the nature of the work does not lend itself to the achievement of economies of scale.

Some industries provide highly individualistic or 'exclusive' items. Such items are generally luxury goods and if produced on a large scale would lose their attraction as their appeal is their uniqueness. Such goods will frequently be the creations of talented, individuals and as the supply of such people is limited, the firm is unlikely to grow to large scale. Examples include designing, architecture and high fashion.

Small firms may survive in an industry by locating a **specialised segment of the market** which does not interest the large manufacturer who prefers longer production runs.

In the engineering industry many small firms survive by taking **work which is subcontracted** to them by larger firms who have no spare capacity and have too much work, or where the small firm provides a specialised service to the larger firms. Small firms may also undertake the highly specialised 'one-off' jobs that are of no interest to the larger firms.

Large firms may allow small firms to exist in order to **prevent investigation by the Monopolies Commission** (Chapter 18).

The fact that a firm is small may merely be due to the fact that it is in an **early stage of its growth** and is one of the large firms of tomorrow.

Economies of scale undoubtedly give advantages to larger firms, but there is little doubt that there will always be a place for the small enterprising firm, and it may be the case that such firms offer the greatest prospects for economic growth.

Self assessment questions

1 What are the two main methods by which firms grow?

2 Distinguish between vertical and horizontal integration.

3 What is meant by internal economies of scale?

4 What are the main motives for horizontal integration?

5 Give four examples of internal economies of scale.

6 Why do small firms survive despite the economies of scale enjoyed by large firms?

11

Business units and sources of capital

1 Business units and capital

The oldest and simplest form of business unit is the **sole proprietor**, a single individual providing all the capital, running the business, accepting all the risk and taking any profits which arise. The growth of specialisation and division of labour and the increased use of mechanised production however, increased both the demand for capital and the need for more specialisation within the management of businesses. The growing demand for capital in particular during the 19th century was a major factor in the development of **joint stock companies**. In joint stock companies the capital, for the acquisition of machines, premises and other assets, is raised from shareholders who each purchase shares in the business in return for a share of the profit, or dividend, at the end of the trading period. In this way joint stock companies are able to raise large amounts of capital to facilitate the growth of the business; by utilising the available reserves of numerous individuals, who individually may only be able to make a small contribution, but collectively the amount of available capital may be substantial.

2 Legal personality

Joint stock companies are a separate entity from the shareholders who own the business and in law have a **legal personality distinct from the owners**. This gives the firm all the rights in law of an individual, to sue or be sued etc. Such organisations are referred to as **corporate bodies**, hence joint stock companies are sometimes referred to as **corporations.** Because the shares are on sale to the general public they may also be referred to as **public companies**.

3 Limited liability

The ever growing demand for capital in the 19th century as production methods became larger, more complex, and therefore more expensive, meant that if firms were to develop the new technology and continue to grow then new sources of capital had to be found, in particular the funds of those with small amounts of wealth who were not prepared to take the risk of losing their investment in the event of the firms bankruptcy. This resulted in the mid 19th century in the introduction of **limited liability**. With limited liability companies the liability of the shareholder is limited in the sense that in the event of the firm going bankrupt they stand **only to lose the amount of their original investment and no more.** In this way firms are able to attract the small saver, who is more averse to risk taking, into investing in shares. As a result, corporations have access to far greater sources of funds than smaller business units. The owners of the business, the shareholders, however, have little control over the running of the business which is in the hands of paid managers.

4 Conglomerates

Established joint stock companies have a tendency to grow in size by acquiring, or merging with, other companies and may eventually become large **conglomerates** producing wide ranges of products or multinational with subsidiaries in many countries. The growth of companies is described in more detail in Chapter 10.

5 Business structures

The sole trader and the public joint stock company represent the smallest and largest of the business units and between their two extremes there are a number of intermediate forms through which business may grow. The actual choice of business unit will depend upon the financial, legal and organisational requirements of the firm. The main business units and their characteristics are outlined below, however it is frequently the case that a firm may start initially as sole proprietor or partnership and develop through the other stages into a joint stock company as the need for capital and more specialised management becomes greater as a consequence of the growth of the business.

6 The sole trader

The sole trader (proprietor) is the oldest and still the most common form of business unit. Many types of business find the sole trader a useful form of business organisation, for example shop-keepers and various services, such as; accountants, solicitors, window cleaners and painters. It is particularly prevalent in the retail trade.

The advantages of the sole trader are:

- The proprietor is their **'own boss'** and has complete control over the business.
- The **rewards of the business belong to the proprietor.** Therefore all profits belong to the proprietor.
- The proprietor is able to **choose all products they wish** to trade in and how they wish to trade in those goods, without consulting any other person.
- The sole trader can offer a **personal service.**

The **disadvantages** of a sole trader are:

- **Unlimited liability,** i.e. the debts of the business are not regarded as separate from the debts of the individual and in the event of financial difficulties, creditors will be able to claim the person's individual assets in settlement of their debt, e.g. house, car, etc.

- The sole traders **bear all the risks themselves** and are unable to have the benefit of spreading the risk of decision making amongst other people.
- The sole trader may be limited in the ability to expand owing to a **lack of capital**.
- One person may also be **restricted in the number of suitable business ideas** they are able to develop. Even if they have good ideas, time may be a constraint on development.

7 Partnerships

Partnerships can be of two types although the ordinary or general partnership is by far the most common. The two forms of partnership are:

- **The ordinary partnership**, which is governed by the Partnership Act 1890.
- **Limited partnerships**, governed by the Limited Partnership Act 1907.

The limited partnership is a rare type of organisation since it yields few benefits which cannot be more easily obtained through limited company status.

There must be between two and twenty partners, except for certain types of professional partnership such as firms of accountants and solicitors.

Partners' rights, responsibilities and rewards are normally specified in a legal document called **'the partnership deed'**. In the absence of such a deed (which is not required by law), the rights rewards and responsibilities of each of the partners is determined by the **Partnership Act 1890.**

All partners may take part in the management and running of business in this type of organisation. As a result, the partners are 'jointly and severally' liable for any debts incurred by partnership.

Limited partnerships arise where a partner known as the **'sleeping partner'** or a limited partner wishes to invest in the business but has no desire to take part in the running of the business his only reward is to receive a proportion of the profits as determined by agreement. A limited partner is not allowed to take part in the management of the business by law (Limited Partnership Act).

The **advantages** of partnership are as follows:

- More than one person is able to make decisions and share in the decision making process.
- Normally there are a small number of people to consult when deciding on new products, or what products to trade in.
- Partnerships may also be able to offer a personal service, i.e facilitates a degree of specialisation within the management of the business. For example, one partner may specialise in finance and the other in marketing.

The **disadvantages** of partnerships are as follows:

- Partners may disagree.
- If one partner decides to leave the partnership, the partnership must be dissolved, i.e. there is no continuity.
- There may be a limit to the amount of capital available for expansion.

8 Partnership limitations

A partnership is not a legal entity, i.e. it is not recognised as a person in law, but it is regarded as an association of individuals. This has the following consequences:

- The firm cannot sue or be sued in its own name, any legal action must be taken by or against any or all of the partners.
- It cannot contract in its own name.
- On the withdrawal of a partner, either voluntarily or upon death or bankruptcy, the partnership is terminated.
- In the event of insolvency, i.e. the business going bankrupt, any or all of the partners can be held liable to contribute to the deficiency from his or her private estate.
- Any partner acting with authority as a representative of the business binds his fellow partners in contract.
- A partner may not transfer his share of the business without the consent of his fellow partners.

9 Limited companies

Limited companies (joint stock companies), have the following characteristics:

- **Limited liability**. A member's liability is limited to any amount unpaid on his shares i.e. a shareholder in the event of liquidation would lose only the amount paid or payable for the shares he owns, unlike a partnership or sole trader, his personal assets will not be used in the settlement of outstanding debts of the business.
- **Legal entity**. A company is regarded as a 'person' at law, i.e. the business is separate from the owners of the business (divorce of ownership from control). Thus a company may contract in its own name.
- **Continuity**. The existence of a company is not affected by any change in its members, no matter how much its ownership changes by the transfer of shares, the company remains unaltered.

10 Public and private companies

Public and private companies are registered companies and are the most common type of company in the UK. They have the following characteristics:

- Any company must have at least **two members,** there is no **maximum**.
- A public company must state in its **memorandum of association** that it is a public company and it must be registered as such.
- A private company is a company which is not a public company (cannot trade on the stock exchange).
- A public company may invite the public to subscribe for its shares and debentures. A private company may not.
- The shares of a public company are **freely transferable** whereas a shareholder in a private company may have to have **agreement of the other members**.
- A public company must end its name with the words **public limited company** or the abbreviation **plc.**
- A public company must have an authorised **minimum share capital of £50,000.**

- A private company may commence trading immediately it is registered. A public company must first have a **'trading certificate'** after it has proved that the authorised minimum share capital has been taken up.

The disadvantages are having to complete administrative documentation, such as memorandum and articles of association, filing company returns with the registrar and subjecting the business to an annual audit which is required by the Companies Act 1985, and other legal requirements specified therein. These disadvantages have to be weighed against the overriding advantage which is to limit the liability of the members.

11 Regulations for limited companies

Internal and external regulations for limited companies are:

- The Memorandum of Association establishes the legal identity of the company and determines and limits objects. Any activity of the company or its directors beyond scope of the objects is **'ultra-vires'** (outside the powers).
- The **Articles of Association** are the internal rules for governing the conduct of the company. They will include regulations establishing the powers, rights and obligations of members and directors. They may be altered within the bounds of the law, with the agreement of the holders of 75% of the voting shares.
- The **Companies Act 1985** consists of extensive legislation, supported by a considerable amount of case law. The 1985 Act consolidated the previous Companies Acts into a single Act and established the legal framework for the running of companies.
- The **Stock Exchange Regulations** regulate the dealing in shares on the Stock Exchange. Shares in public companies may be dealt in on the Stock Exchange only if they have been admitted to the listing. The 'permission to deal' granted by the Stock Exchange imposes on a company and its directors, regulations stricter than those required by law. The main purpose of this is to give additional protection to shareholders and investors.

12 Ownership and control

As a consequence of the fact the limited (or joint stock) companies have their capital subscribed by shareholders there is **a separation between the ownership and the running of the business by its management**. They are therefore:

- **Owned** by the shareholders.
- **Managed** by the directors.
- **Controlled** by those holding a majority of the voting shares because those shareholders can determine who are to be the directors.

13 Capital sources

Joint stock companies can therefore raise their capital by the sale of shares to the public. In the case of public companies shares may be traded on the **stock exchange** provided they have a Stock Exchange listing. Unlisted companies may have their shares traded on the **unlisted securities market**, which has undergone rapid growth over recent years; and is generally used by smaller companies. Shares may be purchased for two reasons; for a steady income from the dividends, or to make a capital gain by buying them at one price and re-selling them later at a higher price. As far as the firm is concerned, after it has raised its initial capital, it is of little consequence if its shares are later resold on numerous occasions, all it requires is the name and address of the current owner in its share register in order to send the dividend to the owner of the share. Shares may be purchased by individuals but are also purchased by various institutions such as insurance companies, unit trust companies, pension funds, finance houses etc. as part of their portfolio of assets. The trend in the UK has been towards institutional ownership of firms with over 80% of shares in 1995 owned by institutions and less than 20% by private individuals.

14 Nationalised industries

In the UK the government itself is responsible for a substantial proportion of output. This **public sector** activity may carried out directly by a central government department, or by local government. In some cases however, the type of activity may resemble more closely the activity and output of a private sector commercial enterprise. Where such industries, for either economic political, or strategic reasons, are owned by the state they are referred to as **nationalised industries**.

15 Organisation of public corporations

The nationalised industries in Britain were run by **public corporations** which were established by an Act of Parliament. These public sector corporations differed from those in the private sector mainly from the point of view of ownership and control. Public corporations had only a single owner which was the state, unlike the private sector corporation which is privately owned by shareholders. Each public corporation was slightly different in organisation of its internal structure but they were generally under control of a **chairman** and a **board** who were appointed by the appropriate minister, e.g. Secretary of State for Industry, Energy or Transport. The corporations were nominally free from interference by the minister in the day to day running of the industry which was intended to be left to the management, although governments sometimes found it difficult to resist interfering when they had some broader objective in mind, for example, dictating pricing policy during a period of inflation.

16 Control of public corporations

Public corporations were not subject to control through a meeting of shareholders at an annual general meeting in the way that a private corporation is; instead external control was exercised in three ways:

- **Ministerial control** through appointments to the board and general powers of direction. The minister also had the power to demand information and then control over specific areas designated under the act which nationalised the industry.
- **Parliamentary control,** indirectly through the minister and also parliamentary procedure, in particular the select committees known as the Public Accounts Committee and the Nationalised Industry Committee, which examined the financial reports and accounts of the nationalised industries.

- **Consumer councils** existed for each of the industries, they are intended to act as channels of communications for the opinions of the consumers of the industries goods and services regarding the standards of provision.

17 Control of the privatised utilities

The nationalised industries have since 1979 been returned to private ownership, as indicated in Chapter 1. The privatisation of these state owned monopolies leaves them with a structure similar to that for any public company as described above. In the case of the privatised utilities such as water, gas, electricity and telecommunications, however there are still the remaining problems which follow from the creation of a monopoly supplier of an essential utility. The problem becomes that of how to obtain the benefits of privatisation in terms of costs and efficiency whilst at the same time protecting the interests of consumers. It is for this reason that the concept of regulated companies was introduced. The activities of the privatised utilities are subject to a degree of regulation regarding the maintenance of quality and their pricing strategies. The major agencies in the UK are:

- Office of Telecommunication (OFTEL)
- Office of Water Services (OFWAT)
- Office of Electricity Regulation (OFFER)
- Office of Gas Supply (OFGAS).

The Monopolies and Mergers Commission (MMC) is also involved in regulation because of the monopoly position held by these utilities. The determination of prices by the regulatory bodies can be subject to appeal to the MMC.

Regulation, therefore, is intended to balance the requirements of ownership and efficiency with the public interest.

Self assessment questions

1 Distinguish between a private and public company.

2 What is meant by limited liability?

3 What are the main disadvantages of partnership as a business unit?

4 How do joint stock companies raise their capital?

5 In what sense does a company have a legal personality?

6 Distinguish between private and public corporations with regard to ownership and control.

7 What is meant by regulation and why is it considered necessary?

Sources of capital

1 Sources

Firms require fixed capital for the replacement or expansion of fixed assets such as plant and premises and working capital for acquisition of stock and meeting the costs of production. Sources of funds are therefore required which are **short term** and **long term** and may be generated from both **internal, external sources**.

2 Internal sources

Internal sources are the major source of funds for industrial and commercial companies in the United Kingdom. Internal funds are provided from retained profits and provisions for depreciation. In established companies these account for approximately two thirds of the total requirements and are therefore also the most important source of long term funds.

3 External sources

The major source of **external** funds for joint stock companies is the **shareholders' capital**. Shareholders' funds will include the funds raised by the company by the issue of shares at the commencement of the business. This is generally referred to as the issued share capital. Many companies when commencing however, will have **authorised share capital** which may be much higher than the share capital which is initially issued. If at some future date it should need extra funds to finance a major new project then it can issue the extra shares in order to raise the required capital. When the issue of new shares are restricted to the existing shareholders they are referred to as a **rights issue**, and may be issued at a price below the current market price. The shares of the public companies are traded on the **Stock Exchange** which is a medium for raising finance for the larger public companies with a Stock Exchange listing. Those companies unable to afford the high costs of a Stock Exchange listing and not wishing to meet the requirement to make a minimum of 25% of the company's share available to the public, may use the unlisted securities market where the costs of issue are much lower and only 10% of the company's shares need to be made available to the public.

4 Shares

Shares can be of several different types and a company will generally issue some, or all, of the following choices:

Ordinary shares (equities). This class of share bears the highest risk as they are entitled to a share of the profits as determined by the directors only when all the other classes of shareholder have been paid. They may receive no dividend if the directors deem it necessary to retain profit in the business for expansion or to create an accumulated fund as a precaution against bad years. On the other hand, ordinary shareholders may do very well in exceptionally good years. Ordinary shareholders have full voting rights at the annual general meeting and therefore have the right to appoint or dismiss the members of the board of directors.

Preference shares carry a fixed rate of dividend payable before the ordinary shareholders are paid. The preference shares can be classified into categories, each one indicating priority of payment. For example, Class A shares might be paid before Class B and so on. If the company has incurred arrears on preference shares because it had insufficient profits to pay in a previous year, then these must be paid before any ordinary dividends are paid. All preference shares are **cumulative** unless otherwise stated, i.e. if the firm is unable to pay a dividend one year, owing to insufficient net profits being earned, two years' dividends fall due in the next year. Preference shareholders do not have voting rights.

- Preference shares may be non cumulative.
- Participating preference shares carry a right to a fixed dividend plus a share of the profits available to ordinary shareholders.
- Redeemable preference shares are the only type of non-permanent share. The company gives an undertaking to redeem shares at a specified time, often at a premium.

5 Debentures

Debentures form an alternative source of long term external finance. Debentures are not shares but are more in the nature of a **long term loan** to companies in return for a **fixed rate of interest** which is irrespective of the profit made by the company. The debenture is a document issued by the company as evidence of the loan. It is redeemable after a specified period, for example 20 years; after which it must be repaid. Debentures are virtually free of risk because if the company is unable to meet its interest or repay the loan, the debenture holder can force the company into liquidation. Holders of **mortgage debentures** are in the position of **secured creditors** in that the loan is secured against specified assets of the company which the debenture holders can force the company to liquidate (sell) in order to meet its commitment. As debentures are loans rather than shares, debenture holders do not have voting rights. In the event of liquidation they are paid out before trade creditors and shareholders.

6 Loan finance

The major source of external loan finance for the short term requirements of most businesses is the banks. Bank borrowing accounts for approximately 60% of the external funds of UK industrial and commercial companies. Borrowing from the banks can either be by loan or by overdraft.

Banks are the major source of short-term finance for most businesses. Bank loans are generally used for specific purposes, and in particular for the acquisition of fixed assets, for example, plant and equipment. The bank will charge an arrangement or negotiation fee, and interest on the loan. Over the period of the loan, the charges made in interest will be greater than the arrangement fee. Loan interest is normally repayable on the capital or on the balance outstanding at between 2% and 5% above the banks base rate. All the major clearing banks' base rates, i.e. National Westminster, Barclays, Lloyds, the Midland and Royal Bank of Scotland, tend to move in line with each other. Most banks providing loans will require security, which is normally in the form pledging assets of the business; in other words, the loan will be secured against either what is called a fixed charge, that is a particular asset, for example, a motor vehicle, a machine, a factory; or a floating charge where the loan is secured against any asset that the firm holds. In the case of a floating charge, if the bank decides to call in its loan then it is entitled to recover the value of the loan and any interest due up to that date by means of selling any asset to the equivalent value that the firm has. In the case of a fixed charge, the bank has the right to sell the particular asset against which the loan is secured, take the amount that is due to the bank, and give the remainder back to the liquidator who is then able to repay other creditors.

Overdraft facilities are granted by negotiation with the firm's branch manager. Loans are normally for a specific purpose, whereas overdrafts are to meet any short term cash crisis. The overdraft facility is normally in existence for a long period of time. Interest on an overdraft is always paid on the amount of money actually borrowed, and this is calculated on a daily basis by the bank. Overdrafts are normally cheaper than loans because the interest rate charges are normally between $1\frac{1}{2}$% to $4\frac{1}{2}$% above the bank's base rate (i.e. the base lending rate plus $1\frac{1}{2}$% to $4\frac{1}{2}$%). From the borrower's point of view, bank overdrafts are a very flexible way of financing short term because the low interest rates are attractive. However, the danger is that the business becomes reliant on the overdraft, and furthermore from the banker's point of view, the overdraft is legally repayable on demand, therefore the bank could ask for repayment of the overdraft immediately. Normally, however, the bank will agree that an overdraft shall not be called in for a defined period of time and generally banks are prepared to continue financing a client whose business it considers to be profitable, and is showing a regular turnover of funds, but is in need of temporary finance owing to cash flow difficulties. From the bank's point of view, they would much prefer a self-liquidating loan, in other words, they would like to lend funds for a specific project which will yield a cash return which is able to meet their repayment. In order to obtain any form of loan from a bank, it will be essential that the business produces a cash flow forecast together with a profit forecast showing its ability to repay the loan or the overdraft in question.

7 Venture capital

In addition to the sources described above, there are also a variety of institutions which will provide venture capital for organisations, most of them being government sponsored. These bodies include: The Industrial and Commercial Finance Corporation (ICFC), Technical Development Capital Ltd., Finance For Industry (FFI), The National Research Development Corporation (NRDC) and Equity Capital for Industry. These organisations generally provide loans and advice, usually to smaller firms; and in particular where technological innovation is involved.

8 Loans and equity finance

The choice between loans and equity finance will be influenced by the relative costs of the two sources. Equity finance may be more expensive because equity holders who accept a higher risk (they may not receive a dividend in any particular year) will require a higher average rate of return than loan finance which would be considered to be more certain and therefore safer. Also the interest paid on the loan stock is an allowable expense on the company's tax liability. A further reason for preferring loan finance is that the issue of additional equity will result in a further dilution of the company's ownership. The ratio of debt to equity finance is referred to as **gearing** and is expressed by:

$$\text{Gearing} = \frac{\text{Debt}}{\text{Equity}} = \frac{\text{Long term debt and preference shares}}{\text{Equity capital}}$$

A highly geared company is one which has a high proportion of debt to equity and vice versa. The level of gearing affects the overall cost of finance to the firm, although under highly restrictive conditions, Modigliani and Miller have shown that the level of gearing is neutral regarding the firms cost of finance.

Self assessment questions

1 Distinguish between ordinary shares, preference shares, debentures.

2 What are the major sources of external finance available to a firm?

3 What is meant by the term 'gearing' in the context of a firm's financial structure?

References

1 *Modigliani, F and Miller, M.H. 'The Cost of Capital, Corporation Finance and the Theory of Investment' AER Vol 48 (1958).*

13

Location of production

1 Location decisions

The choice of site at which to locate may have a significant affect upon the firm's costs, and it is important, in theory at least, that the firm selects a site which minimises the costs associated with location. In reality however the choice of site may also be influenced by other factors which are not necessarily economic and modern industries may have a considerable degree of freedom in the decision as to the best site at which to locate.

2 Transport costs

Transport costs were considered to be an important factor in determining location, although they have less significance today than in the past. The transport of either raw materials or finished goods can have a considerable influence upon the final cost of a product. There are two opposing influences in this context, on the one hand the firm will desire to be as close as possible to its sources of **raw materials** but at the same time will wish to be as close as possible to the **market** for its final product and these two requirements may frequently oppose one another, being closer to raw materials may leave the firm more distant from its markets. This is sometimes explained in terms of '**weight gaining**' and '**weight losing**' processes. Some materials lose weight during the manufacturing process, for example, flour milling, iron ore refining and sugar beet refining. Others gain weight during processing, for example, prefabricated buildings, brewing and engineering. When a product loses weight during manufacturing it will tend to gravitate towards the source of raw material in order to minimise transport costs. An example is iron ore, which in the UK tends to have a low yield, has traditionally been smelted in the areas where it is quarried; in Northamptonshire and Lincolnshire. Flour milling is commonly carried out at ports for the same reason. In some cases the extraction or refining process has been shifted to the primary producing country; in particular the extraction of edible oils from seeds and palm kernel has shifted from the UK back to the producer countries such as Nigeria, where the oil is extracted and only the refined oil shipped to the UK. This reduces the transport costs but also gives a greater 'value added' for the producer country. Weight gaining processes are those where the product gains weight during the production process and in such cases the cost of transport will be minimised by locating closer to the market place. The extreme example would be prefabricated buildings which are assembled on site. Brewing was originally carried out in town centre breweries as it was more economic to distribute the finished product over as short a distance as possible to the largest market. Changes in brewing technology and transport have however considerably changed the location requirements of the brewing industry. Theoretically therefore the firm will choose an optimal location, which will be the one that minimises its transport costs given the extent to which its product gains or loses weight during the manufacturing process. This site may be at the source of the raw material, the final market, or some intermediate point.

The analysis of location according to the degree of weight gain or loss can be criticised on the grounds that it is the ratio of unit value to weight of the product which is more important than the actual weight. Where products have a low value to weight ratio then transport is likely to be a far more important consideration than for products with a high value to weight ratio. The example of beer brewing quoted earlier is a product with a low value to weight ratio hence transport constitutes a higher proportion of total cost, and the firm will attempt to minimise transport costs by locating as close to the market as possible. Where products have a high value to weigh ratio transport becomes a minor factor, as it is a low proportion of total cost, and location is less critical, for example, whisky can be distilled in Scotland and sold worldwide.

3 Sources of power

Proximity to sources of power was an important factor in determining location during the 19th and early 20th centuries. Early industry was located near fast moving rivers when water power was the prime source of power, later water power was superseded by steam power and nearness of a supply of coal became important hence industry became concentrated on the coalfields of the north of England. Since the widespread adoption of electricity which is available almost everywhere in the UK through the National Grid, it is no longer necessary for the supply of a power source to have influence over the location of the firm.

4 Declining influences

Improvements in transport and availability of power have mean that access to raw materials and power are now of minor importance in the firm's location decision and many industries are now described as '**footloose**', meaning that they can locate virtually anywhere they choose.

5 Access to markets

Access to markets is now one of the most important factors influencing the location decision. This has always been the case with goods where the ratio of value to transport costs is low or for goods which are perishable, for example, ice-cream has always been produced close to large centres of population. However, with the major changes which have taken place in the industrial structure and the methods of transport **market access has**

become a dominant factor. Much of UK industrial output today consists of lighter high value goods such as electronics, which are easily transportable and consequently has low transport costs, and transport is therefore a relatively unimportant factor. Ease of access to large markets such as the cities may figure more significantly in the location decision. This tendency has been accelerated by technical improvements in transport with larger vehicles, containerisation, improved mechanical handling, and the development of the motorway system. Many of the newer lighter industries therefore tend to be near to the big conurbations, in particular in the south east in proximity to London and in the Midlands. It is also interesting to note the proliferation of industrial estates around the access points to motorways in order to take advantage of the shorter delivery times and ease of access offered by the motorway system. Access to large trading blocks such as the EU may also be a factor in location, for example, the decision by the Japanese car manufacturers Nissan to locate in the north-east of England was partly influenced by the desire to obtain access to EU countries for the marketing of their vehicles.

6 Labour

Labour requirements can also influence the firm's location, in particular the need for specific types of labour. For example, a firm in the cotton textile industry would find the skilled labour it required by locating in Lancashire; this readily available skilled labour force would have the effect of reducing the firm's training costs. Much of industry is however now much less labour intensive, utilising more capital intensive methods of production and requiring less skilled labour. Many firms now require unskilled or semi-skilled labour and do not want permanent commitments to the labour force. They may therefore prefer to employ part-time female labour, nearness to large urban areas is therefore attractive to many firms, particularly those involved in light assembly work. As consequence, many industries are now 'footloose' regarding the labour requirements.

7 Industrial inertia

Originally the location of an industry in a particular area may have been due to certain natural advantages which the area could offer, for example the damp atmosphere of Lancashire was a attraction to the cotton spinning industry as it prevented the threads from snapping, steel making at Sheffield due to the availability of coal and iron. These factors may no longer be as relevant today as technology has superseded the original advantages, as in the case of artificial humidifiers in the cotton industry, however the industry may remain in the same area due to **industrial inertia**. Industrial inertia keeps an industry in an area long after the original advantages have been lost. This is due to certain **acquired advantages** which offer **external economies of scale** to the industry, for example a skilled labour force or suppliers of components (see Chapter 9).

8 Non economic factors

If we assume that firms attempt to maximise profits then they will at all times select the site which offers the lowest overall cost; in reality however **non-economic factors** may weigh heavily on the decision. Once located in an area, senior management may be reluctant to move to another site which they find less attractive from the point of view of amenities, friends, housing, children's schooling and status. This can explain to some extent the reluctance of firms to move away from the south-east of England to the regions of higher unemployment in the north despite the attraction of government grants. There are also many examples of firms which are located at a particular site for no reason other than the personal preference of the original founder. Morris built his motor car factory at Cowley in Oxford, not for any particular economic advantages but because he happened to live there and the family cycle business was already located in the town.

9 Government policy

Government regional policy can be a further influence in the location decision. Governments offer a range of grants and other incentives to firms in order to attract them to locate in the regions where unemployment is highest.

10 Present trends

The major trend in location today is the increased freedom of firms in the choice of site. Technical developments in production, transport and sources of power have all contributed to making industry more 'footloose' than ever before. This trend has been accelerated by the tendency towards 'disintegration' in some large industries. Disintegration refers to the buying out from suppliers of components and assembling them rather than the firm manufacturing all its own components. This trend is particularly prevalent in the motor car industry where it gives the manufacturer more freedom in the location decision. For example, Ford at Dagenham closed their foundry for making engine blocks as this tied them to one source of supply. Ford and Vauxhall on Merseyside now produce cars from components brought in from plants in various European countries and assemble them on site rather than produce entire vehicles. Modern multi-national companies when looking at the location decision do not feel constrained to a single country but will consider the choice of alternatives on a world-wide basis. The opening of the Channel Tunnel will undoubtedly influence the location decisions of many UK firms in the future as they attempt to minimise their total distribution costs. This may be achieved by locating facilities, particularly distribution centres, either at a convenient point for access to the tunnel or even by establishing distribution centres in European locations.

Self assessment questions

1 How does the concept of weight gaining and weight losing materials affect the firm's location decision?

2 What is meant by an industry being 'footloose'?

3 Why is most industry more footloose now than in the past?

4 What is meant by industrial inertia?

5 How might the advent of the Channel Tunnel influence the location decisions of UK firms?

14

Perfect competition

1 Market forms

We consider next the various market forms, the first of which is **perfect competition**. In reality very few markets are perfectly competitive, examples being the Chicago Grain Market, the Stock Exchange, and some of the commodity markets; however the concept does provide a yardstick by which the degree of competition in real world markets can be measured. It is assumed here that firms compete on price alone and not the other forms of competition, such as advertising, which may be a characteristic of other market forms.

2 Market conditions

In order for a market to be considered as perfectly competitive, a number of conditions must be satisfied, these are:

- There must be a single **homogeneous** (same) **product**, i.e. each seller is offering an identical product.
- There must be **many buyers and sellers**, none of whom can alone influence the market price.
- All buyers and sellers must have **perfect information** regarding the market.
- **Perfect mobility of factors of production** to and from the industry. If profits are high, entrepreneurs can enter the industry, or leave if greater returns can be earned elsewhere.

Given these conditions, there can only be a single market price which cannot be influenced by the activities of any single buyer or seller. As competition is based purely on price, and the product is homogeneous, buyers will buy from whoever is the cheapest; therefore each producer is forced to adopt the least-cost method of production and all excess profits or losses will in the long run be eliminated by entry to, or exit from, the industry.

3 Perfectly elastic demand

We can illustrate the concept by using a simple diagram. In Figure 14.1 we have a buyer in a market place where there are six sellers all selling an identical product, say for example, bags of sugar. The buyer knows the price each seller is charging and we assume that the buyer behaves in a rational manner.

Assume that seller 1 raises his price while the others all keep theirs constant, clearly the buyer will buy zero from seller 1 and obtain his requirements from the others. On the other hand, if seller 1 reduced his price whilst the others kept theirs constant, the others would all sell zero and seller 1 would sell all that the buyer was willing to take. This is in fact another way of saying that the firm in perfect competition has an infinitely elastic demand curve (see Chapter 7).

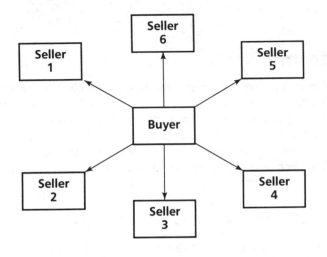

Figure 14.1

4 Revenue

Marginal revenue is the addition to **total revenue** which a firm receives from the sale of one extra unit of output.

The total revenue of the firm (TR) is calculated as **price × quantity**.

Average revenue (AR) is the same as price. This is obvious if we consider that Total Revenue is defined as **price × quantity**.

i.e. $\text{TR} = \text{P} \times \text{Q}$

therefore $\text{AR} = \dfrac{\text{TR}}{\text{Q}} = \text{P}$

if AR = P then the **average revenue** curve is the **same thing as the demand curve**.

5 MR=AR=D

In perfect competition as each unit is sold at the same price then both MR and AR are constant and are the **same as the demand curve**, this is shown more clearly in Table 14.1 where it can be seen that because price is constant, under conditions of perfect competition

$P = AR = Dd = MR$. This is illustrated graphically in Figure 14.2. (Marginal revenue under conditions of imperfect competition where the demand curve is downward sloping is illustrated in Appendix 1 on page 99.)

Table 14.1				
P	Q	TR	AR (TR) / Q	MR (Increase in Total Revenue)
5	1	5	5	
				5
5	2	10	5	
				5
5	3	15	5	
				5
5	4	20	5	
				5
5	5	25	5	
				5
5	6	30	5	

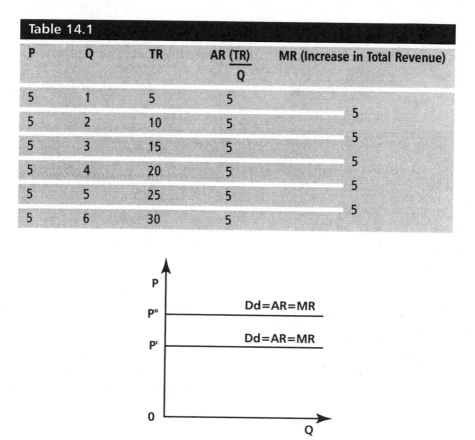

Figure 14.2

The firm's demand curve, as stated above, is infinitely elastic so it can sell all its output at the prevailing market price. The price, in this case P' in Figure 14.2, is determined by the market and cannot be influenced by the individual firm whose output is too small relative to the total industry output. The firm in perfect competition is therefore said to be a **'price taker'** rather than a 'price maker'.

6 Price determination

The equilibrium market price, which applies to each firm, is determined by the intersection of the market demand and supply curves for the **industry as a whole**. The industry demand curve slopes downwards because if the industry as a whole reduces its price it will sell more. The industry or market equilibrium price, P' in Figure 14.3, is at the point where the market demand and supply curves intersect. This establishes the price for every firm in the industry. Should the market price fall or rise for any reason, this new price will then apply to every firm in the industry. For example, an increase in industry demand to D′ in Figure 14.3 increases the price for each firm in the industry to P″; in Figure 14.2.

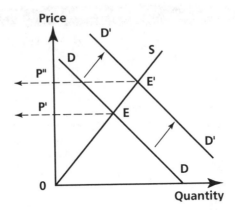

Figure 14.3

7 Profit maximising output

It is now possible to derive the competitive firm's **profit maximising output**. The competitive firm's Average Cost (AC) curve is the usual U-shaped curve, and is of course defined so as to include **normal profit**. The MC falls and then rises sharply cutting AC at its lowest point. In order to maximise its profits, the competitive firm will expand output to the point where MR = MC, at point E, in Figure 14.4. This is the competitive firm's equilibrium point with the profit maximising output at Qe. At lower outputs the firm is not maximising its profits, for example at output Q^2 MR exceeds MC by A–B and the firm

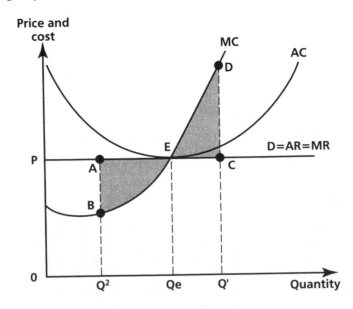

Figure 14.4

can increase its profits by the shaded area by raising its output to Qe. At higher outputs than Qe the firm can increase its profits by reducing output, for example at output Q^1 MC exceeds MR by D–C and the firm is therefore making a loss on each additional unit. Profit will therefore be increased by the shaded area if output is reduced to Qe. As the price is just equal to MC at the lowest point of AC, the firm is using its plant at peak efficiency, and is just covering its costs with no abnormal or super-normal profits being earned, only normal profits being made.

The two essential rules to remember are:

- that a firm's profit maximising output is where

$$MR = MC$$

and this is true of firms under any market conditions
- that under conditions of perfect competition, the firm's price is equal to the marginal cost.

$$P = MC$$

8 Super normal profits

Super normal profits (SNP) can only be earned under **conditions of perfect competition in the short run**, during the period of time which it takes for factors of production to enter the industry.

9 Long run equilibrium

We can now analyse the process by which super normal profit or losses, will be eliminated in a perfectly competitive industry in the transition to long run equilibrium.

In Figure 14.5a. a firm has a short run equilibrium output of Q^0 (MR = MC at E), and cost is only OL (Q^0 M) per unit, hence the firm making a super normal profit of PLME. These high profits will attract new entrants to the industry and supply will increase, prices will start to fall and the amount of super normal profit will decline as in 14.5b, however as long as SNP is being earned, entry to the industry will continue until all SNP's have been eliminated and all firms are earning only normal profits, as in 14.5c. This is the long-run equilibrium.

In Figure 14.5d a firm has a short run equilibrium output of (MR = MC at E), but the cost per unit is OS (Q^0 R) and the firm making a loss of PERS, as is each firm in the industry. Firms will leave the industry in search of higher profits elsewhere, supply will fall and prices rise, reducing the size of the loss, as in Figure 14.5e. As long as losses persist, firms will leave the industry until eventually each firm which remains is a marginal firm making only normal profit, as in Figure 14.5c.

In the long run, all excess profits and losses are eliminated and each firm is a marginal firm selling at P = MC. (14.5c.)

A classic example of excess profits being eliminated by competition was the Rubic's Cube where entry to the industry by new firms brought the price down from £5 to £1 in less than a year. The same sort of competition now exists with micro-computers where competition is reducing prices and profit margins rapidly.

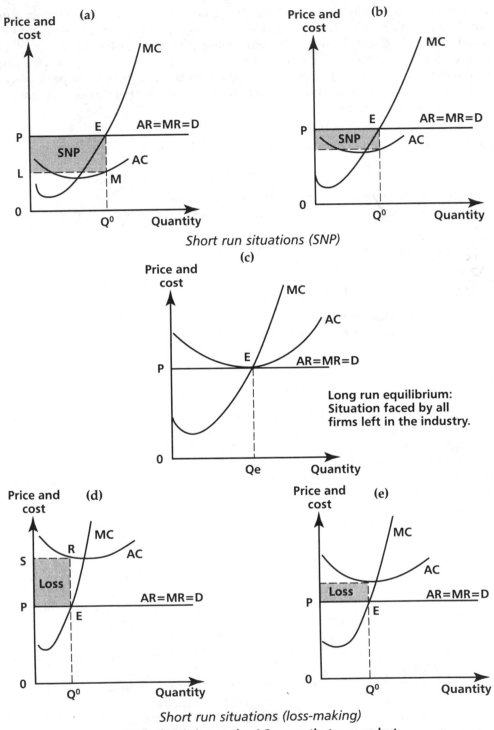

(a)

(b)

Short run situations (SNP)

(c)

Long run equilibrium:
Situation faced by all
firms left in the industry.

(d)

(e)

Short run situations (loss-making)

Note that it is not the AC curve that moves but
the price line AR which moves relative to it

Figure 14.5

10 Normal profit

Although normal profit applies throughout an industry, it is not necessarily the same between different industries. Normal profit can differ between industries due to:

- The degree of risk and uncertainty involved. High risk industries require high profits in order to attract capital.
- The nature of the production process involved. Capital intensive industries require higher rates of return in order to make investment worthwhile.
- Exceptional entrepreneurial ability enables some industries to earn higher profits by skilful management; sometimes referred to as 'rent of ability'.
- There may be quite substantial time lags before firms can enter an industry due to the shortage of skilled labour or the need to construct plant. Such temporary profits are referred to as **quasi rents**, and they occur whenever profits are earned as a result of a temporarily fixed supply of factors of production.

11 Shut-down point

Where firms have specific assets, in the sense that they cannot immediately be used to produce something else if the price of, product falls, they may in fact stay in an industry for a period even if the price falls below average cost. In Figure 14.6 the firm is in equilibrium at E with price P and quantity Q^3. If the price falls to P^1 the firm will move down the MC curve to the new equilibrium of MC = MR and produce Q^2, The firm will continue to produce until price falls to P^2 at which point it will cease production. Equilibrium point M is therefore referred to as the 'shutdown point'. The firm will therefore continue to produce at any price which covers its average variable costs of production, because anything over AVC makes a contribution to the fixed costs which have to be paid whether the firm produces or not, and will therefore reduce the size of its losses. However, if the price falls below its AVC by producing the firm will actually increase its losses, and the more it produces the greater the loss will be. In the short run, therefore, a firm with specific assets will remain in production as long as the price is greater than AVC.

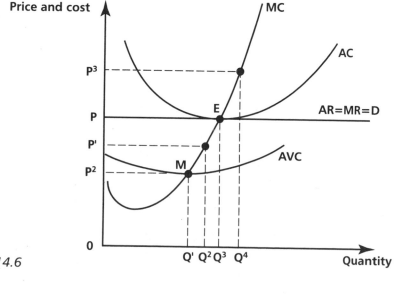

Figure 14.6

12 Marginal cost and supply

If we consider the firm's MC curve in Figure 14.6 it can be observed that the portion of it above M relates the price to the quantity the firm will produce, it is therefore the firm's supply curve. **The competitive firm's MC curve above AVC is its supply curve.** If the MC curves of all the firms in the industry are summed together we obtain the industry supply curve.

13 Imperfect competition

We consider next conditions of **imperfect competition**. The breakdown of perfect competition occurs when one firm introduces a cost saving innovation and is therefore able to produce more cheaply than its competitors. However, not only does it make the innovation, but it is able to keep information regarding the details to itself and permanently undercut its competitors.

Self assessment questions

1 What are the conditions necessary for the existence of a perfectly competitive market?

2 At what point will the perfectly competitive firm be in equilibrium?

3 Where will the perfectly competitive firm in equilibrium set its price?

4 What is meant by normal profit?

5 How are super normal profits eliminated from a competitive industry?

6 Describe the relationship between MC and supply.

7 Under what circumstances may a firm decide to produce and sell at a loss rather than cease production?

Appendix 1

(1) Price (=AR)	(2) Quantity	(3) Total Revenue	(4) Marginal Revenue
20	0	0	
18	1	18	18
16	2	32	14
14	3	42	10
12	4	48	6
10	5	50	2

Because price is not constant where the demand curve is downward sloping AR is not equal to MR. This is discussed further in Chapter 15.

Appendix 2

The firms' profit maximising output can also be determined by the use of **total concepts**. Figure 14.7 illustrates **total cost (TC)** and **total revenue (TR)**. The profit maximising output will be at the point where the difference between TR and TC is the greatest, which coincides with the maximum point on the **total profit curve (TP)**. This profit maximising output is the same as that obtained in the lower section of the diagram by following the MR = MC rule, i.e. OQ. This can be proved by drawing parallel lines at a tangent to TC and TR and these lines will be tangential (touching) TC and TR at the profit maximising output. At this point therefore the rate of change of TR and TC are equal, i.e.

$$\frac{dTR}{dQ} = \frac{dTC}{dQ}$$

and as $\dfrac{dTR}{dQ} = MR$ and $\dfrac{dTC}{dQ} = MC$

then at that output MR = MC (note this proof is not essential for A level or professional students).

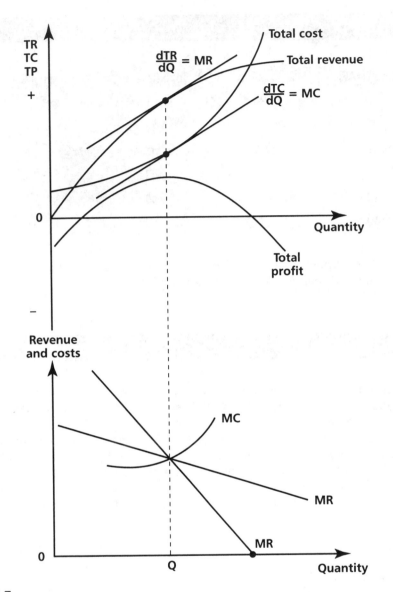

Figure 14.7

Appendix 3

The cost curves actually encountered by firms may not conform exactly to the U-shape predicted by economic theory. In many firms average costs may fall slowly as output increases up to the firm's normal operating capacity, with marginal costs almost constant over the range; as illustrated in Figure 14.8.

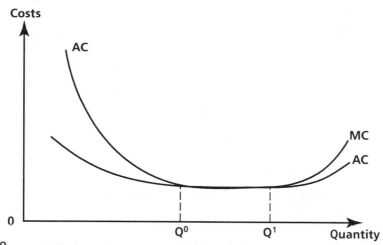

Figure 14.8

The 'normal' operating range is Q^0 to Q^1 and above Q^1 marginal and average costs both rise quite rapidly. Around the normal operating range of Q^0–Q^1, however, costs do not change very much and therefore fluctuations in output around the normal range of output do not have a significant effect upon costs. Also, the whole of the range Q^0–Q^1 can be considered to be the minimum AC, and MC does not cut AC at a single unique point. Cost will, however, be affected by operating at significantly reduced levels of output, or at very high levels of output. In practice, because of the expense involved and the difficulty of obtaining the information, most firms will only bother to estimate their cost curves for a product over a range of output which is relevant to their current level of activity. It is important however to note that the predictions regarding the relationship between average and marginal costs and the fact that they will initially fall and then rise over the total possible range of output are generally valid, although the actual shape of the cost curves may differ between firms.

The model used by cost accountants differs from that used by economists in a number of significant details; the two models can, however, be quite easily reconciled. For practical purposes the cost accountant is only interested in the behaviour of costs and revenue over the range of output which is significant to the firm, i.e. Q^0–Q^1 in Figure 14.8. The cost accounting model assumes that over this range of output variable costs increase proportionately with output, hence the total cost function is a straight line. It is also assumed that the selling price remains constant over this range of output so total revenue rises proportionately with output. Therefore, the total revenue function is also a straight line passing through the origin, as illustrated in Figure 14.9. In the diagram the firm is assumed to 'break-even' at the point where sales revenue is equal to total cost. Profit is the difference between total cost and total revenue, hence above output $\bar{Q}$ the contribution of each unit of output represents additional profit; below $\bar{Q}$ the contribution is insufficient to cover costs and the firm incurs a loss.

If the economic model is expressed in terms of total cost and total revenue functions as in Figure 14.10, the obvious difference from the accounting version is that these functions are not linear. The shape of the total cost function being influenced initially by increasing returns and then diminishing returns. The total revenue curve reflects the fact that total revenue increases more slowly than sales volume.

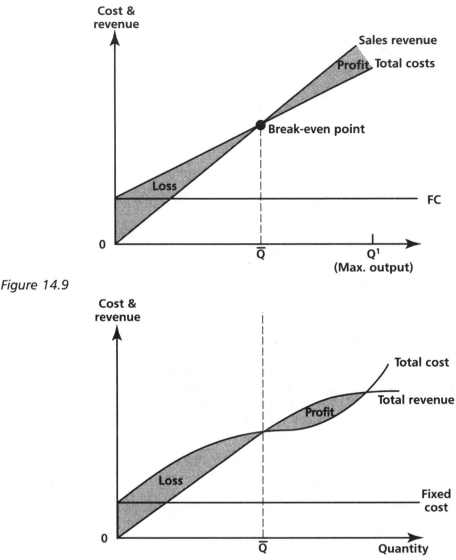

Figure 14.9

Figure 14.10

The main differences between the two versions can be summarised as follows:

- The cost accounting model assumes a constant marginal product, i.e. increasing and diminishing marginal returns are ignored, hence a linear total cost function is utilised.
- The accounting model assumes that all output can be sold at a constant price.

From the economic point of view both of these assumptions are dubious, however the economist is considering the situation over the whole range of possible output whereas the cost accountant is considering the behaviour of costs and revenue over a fairly narrow range of output which is relevant to the firm. The accountant's version provides a practical and simple approach to the determination of costs and output despite its theoretical shortcomings.

15
Monopoly

1 Monopoly market

Monopoly refers to a market where supply is under the control of a single supplier. In the case of perfect monopoly, this will be a single firm, however the effect will be similar if several firms act together in fixing prices, which is referred to as a **cartel**. In both cases buyer is facing a **single source of supply**.

2 Monopoly demand

As the monopolist is the sole source of supply in a market, the demand curve is also the industry demand curve; the monopolist therefore faces a **downward sloping demand curve**. If the monopolist wants to sell more the price must be reduced.

3 Average and marginal revenue

Figure 15.1 illustrates the downward sloping demand curve of the monopolist. It also illustrates another important difference between the monopolist and the competitive

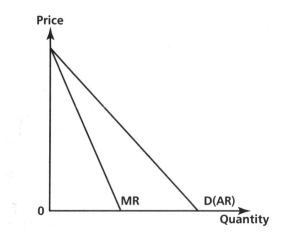

Figure 15.1

firm; the monopolists average revenue (AR) is not the same as marginal revenue (the MR is in fact less than AR.) This is because when the monopolist wants to sell more the price must be reduced, not only on the extra units he sold, but also on all of the earlier units. To illustrate assume that a monopolist is selling 10 units at £1 each, therefore TR = £10. In order to increase his sales to 11 units the price must be reduced to 99p each, and TR = 10.89, i.e. 11 × 99p. The increase in total revenue (TR) from the sale of the extra unit was 89p, despite the price being 99p. This is because of the 1p lost on each of the 10 units sold previously. Mathematically MR has twice the slope of AR (see appendix).

4 Profit maximising output

The monopolist, like any other firm, finds its profit maximising output where MR = MC, at point E in Figure 15.2, giving output OQ̄. Price is however set above the marginal cost of production at M, the appropriate point on the monopolist's demand curve. At output OQ̄ however, the average cost of production is only N, producing a **monopoly profit** (or **monopoly rent**) of PCNM. Unlike the super normal profits earned under perfect competition these monopoly profits will persist into the long run and will not be eliminated by entry to the industry.

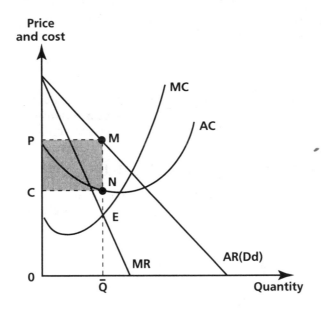

Figure 15.2

5 The case against monopoly

From Figure 15.2 is can also be seen that the monopolist, unlike the competitive firm, is not operating at the lowest point on the AC curve, and could in fact be producing more at a lower cost, but does not choose to do so. Instead the monopolist restricts output and sets price above the marginal cost of production. The monopolist's resources could be used more efficiently elsewhere, hence society's resources are being misallocated. The two arguments against monopoly are therefore:

- They exploit the consumer by setting a price greater than MC.
- They create a loss of efficiency by misallocating societies resources.

It is these two points which frequently lead governments to take action in order to control or curb monopoly power.

6 Taxing monopoly profits

It is sometimes argued that a lump sum tax should be levied upon monopolists equivalent to their monopoly profit which could then be redistributed (i.e. PCNM in Figure 15.2), this would leave their profit maximising equilibrium point E unchanged, and therefore their output. This suggestion however does not overcome the chief objection to monopoly – that of resource misallocation, as monopolist would still not be operating at the most efficient point on the AC curve.

7 Elasticity

Marginal revenue is related to elasticity. Whenever MR is positive demand is elastic, and whenever MR is negative, i.e. below price P in Figure 15.3, demand is inelastic. Monopolists therefore will never produce at a price where demand is inelastic, because the MR is negative and they can increase their total revenue by reducing output.

8 Monopoly power

The monopolist's power will depend upon two factors:

- The availability of substitutes. The greater the absence of substitutes, the greater the power of the monopolist to make profits.
- The ease with which the monopolist can erect **barriers to entry**, to prevent new firms entering the industry (see Chapter 16).

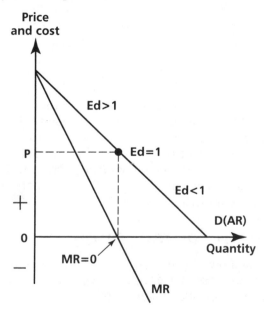

Figure 15.3

9 Limits of monopoly power

The monopolist's power however does not extend to the control of demand. Because the monopolist cannot control demand there are two options:

- Control supply and let demand determine price.
- Set the price and let demand determine the quantity supplied.
- It is not possible, however, to do both.

10 Price discrimination

The monopolist can make greater profits by practising **price discrimination**. Price discrimination refers to the charging of different prices in different markets. Price discrimination will be successful under the following conditions:

There must be no 'leakages' between two markets, i.e. consumers must not be able to travel between markets in order to buy in the cheapest, or buy in one market and re-sell in another, such **arbitrage** would eventually equalise the price in both markets. The **segmentation** of markets may be by either:

- **Time.** Usually used in the case of non-storable services, for example, peak and off-peak rail fares and telephone calls.
- **Geographical dispersion**. Where markets are widely dispersed geographically, price discrimination can be practised as long as the price differential is less than the cost of transport between two markets, e.g. the price differential between Rover cars in the UK and Germany was pushed to the point where it became cheaper for UK buyers to import them from Germany.
- **The status of the consumer** may also provide a basis for price discrimination. For example, the elderly may receive low priced fares on public transport or cheaper seats at the cinema or football matches. Children may be charged less for travel and holidays although they consume the same quantities as adults.

Where the elasticity of demand is different in two markets then charging different prices, a high price in the inelastic market and a lower price in the elastic market, will maximise profits. This can be illustrated by the example of a monopolist selling into two distinctly separate markets, A and B in Figure 15.4. In the absence of price discrimination the price in both markets would be Pe, where MR = MC at E in the combined market (A + B) this price however would be too low in market A and too high in market B. If the markets could be separated and prices set appropriate to their individual MR = MC intersections at M, a price of Pa would be set in market A where demand is **inelastic** and Pb in market B where demand is **elastic.** Because a high price is set in the market where demand is inelastic and a low price in that where demand is elastic, total revenue is maximised in both markets. Only a firm in a monopoly situation however, could exploit such a situation.

Price discrimination does not only occur under monopoly however, but may also occur under other forms of imperfect competition.

11 An argument for monopoly

The classical case against monopoly rests upon the assumption that they misallocate society's resources. The analysis so however, has been conducted in static terms, which assumes other factors, such as costs, remain unchanged when an industry is monopolised.

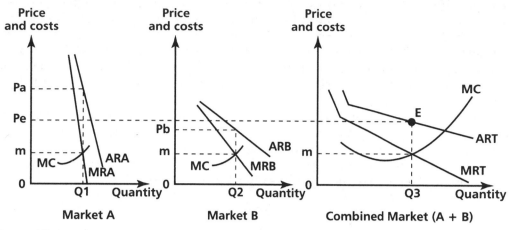

Market A   **Market B**   **Combined Market (A + B)**

Figure 15.4

This may not however be the case and monopolisation may generate dynamic changes which produce benefits to society which outweigh the allocative costs.

12 Monopolisation

Figure 15.5 illustrates the monopolisation of a perfectly competitive industry. Original competitive market demand and supply curves give equilibrium at E at the bottom of each firm's AC curve, with output Qc. After monopolisation of the industry the industry

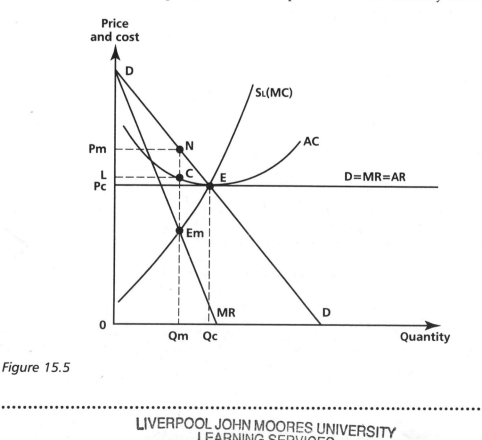

Figure 15.5

demand curve becomes the monopolising firm's demand curve with MR lying below it. Equilibrium of MR = MC is now at Em with output Qm, with price Pm and monopoly profit PmLCN. Output is lower and price higher after the industry has been monopolised. This analysis however assumes that the cost structures remain unchanged, whereas in reality they may well change. The concentration of the production of many small competitive firms may produce such substantial economies of scale that costs will fall as a result.

In Figure 15.6 the competitive industry output is Q with price P. Monopolisation could be expected to reduce output to Q_1 and raise price to P_1. If however monopolisation results in substantial economies of scale which shift costs down from MC to MCm, then the monopolist's output will be higher at Q_2 with the price lower than the competitive price at P_2 despite the existence of monopoly profits.

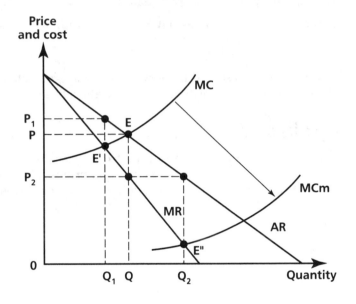

Figure 15.6

13 The benefits of monopoly

Whether monopoly is 'good' or 'bad' must also depend to some extent upon how monopolists actually behave and what they do with the monopoly profits. It is quite possible that the monopolist shares the profits with the workforce in the form of higher than average wage rates and working conditions.

Monopoly profits may also be reinvested within the firm in the form of research and development. An example of this is the drug industry where substantial profits are made, but at the same time the level of research and development into new drugs is high, and most new drugs are in fact introduced by firms with a high degree of market power. Monopoly also avoids the duplication of research and development effort making more efficient use of resources and more rapid technological advancement.

Some authorities such as Joseph Schumpeter and J.P. Galbraith suggest that technical innovation is closely linked to market form and that monopoly is most likely to create the atmosphere which is conducive to innovation. Only monopoly provides the stability in the market which will encourage firms to undertake innovation which is both risky and costly. Only firms making monopoly profits have the resources to undertake extensive research and development, and this will only be undertaken if firms can be certain of achieving a high rate of return on their investment which would by no means be certain in a competitive environment. Monopoly provides the stability and the returns necessary for such expenditures to be undertaken.

Joseph Schumpeter refers to the process of 'creative destruction' in which monopolies make innovations only to eventually have their profits destroyed by competitive activity as the monopolist's profits attract others to try to obtain some for themselves. The classical example of this being the ball point pen which was introduced by the Reynolds Company in 1946, who held a monopoly position at that time. The original price was $12.50 and cost 80c to make; however by 1948 competition had entered the industry and the price fell to 39c and cost 10c to produce, with very little profit left in their production. Patents will not prevent this process as they will be by-passed by the development of similar but slightly different products. Schumpeter estimated that losses due to resource misallocation amounted to no more than 2–3% of national income which was more than outweighed by the increased economic growth generated by innovation.

14 Some conclusions

It is therefore by no means certain that in all cases monopoly is harmful, and even accepting the harmful effects upon resource allocation these allocative costs may be outweighed by benefits of the types described above, a possibility which is reflected in UK legislative controls over monopoly and mergers (see Chapter 18).

Self assessment questions

1 Why is the monopolist's MR less than AR?

2 What are the two main arguments against monopoly?

3 State the conditions which make price discrimination possible.

4 Outline the arguments in favour of monopoly.

5 What factors will determine the market power of a monopolist?

6 What is meant by the process of 'creative destruction'

Appendix

Proof that for the monopolist the marginal revenue curve (MR) has twice the slope of the average revenue curve (AR). Recalling that **AR = Dd = P**. The equation for a downward sloping demand curve, or AR curve is:

(1) $P = a - bq$

where
  a = a constant
  b= the gradient of the curve
  q= quantity demanded.

Total revenue (TR), which is $P \times q$, is obtained therefore by multiplying (1) through by q.

(2) $TR = aq - bq^2$

Marginal revenue refers to a small change in total revenue, so by differentiating total revenue with respect to quantity we obtain marginal revenue.

$$MR = \frac{dTR}{dq} = a - 2bq$$

therefore MR has twice the slope of AR (the coefficient for the gradient is 2b rather than b).

16

Oligopoly

1 A definition

Oligopoly refers to markets which are **dominated by a few sellers** The entire output of the industry is produced by a few large firms and the contribution of each firm is sufficiently large to be significant in the market. Oligopoly is the prevalent market form in many areas of manufacturing in Europe and the UK. The tendency towards oligopoly is a result of the attempts by firms to gain economies of scale by amalgamation and merger. In the UK oligopoly is the characteristic market form in the detergents, car, chemicals and oil industries.

2 Interdependence

Oligopoly is not only distinguished from other market forms by the number of firms but also by a qualitative difference. When the number of competitors in the market are few, each seller becomes acutely aware of how his rivals are likely to react to any change he may make, particularly on price. Oligopoly is the only market form therefore where the firm's pricing and output decisions will also incorporate the perceived, or expected, reactions of competitors. Firms are therefore to a certain extent interdependent, the policies of one influencing the other.

3 Price rigidity

This interdependence helps us to understand one of the major characteristics of oligopoly markets – that of **price rigidity.** The prices charged by monopolists tend to be similar even if there is no collusion (i.e. price fixing). It is necessary therefore to analyse the nature of oligopolistic markets and attempt to identify why it is that the prices charged by the different firms tend to be similar even in the absence of a formal agreement.

4 'Kinked demand curve'

One explanation for this is the **'kinked demand curve'**. This solution suggests that firms in oligopoly potentially face two demand curves, one for price increases which is highly **elastic** and one for price reductions which is highly **inelastic.** In Figure 16.1 for price increases the firm is on the elastic curve dd and for reductions it is on the inelastic curve DD, and the firm's actual demand curve is dED; the demand curve has a 'kink' at E with price $\bar{P}$ and quantity $\bar{Q}$ all the firms in the industry being in a similar position. This is because if one firm raises its price and its competitor fails to follow suit then a large proportion of sales and therefore revenue will be lost, it is therefore on the elastic position of the curve dE. If one firm attempts to reduce price by itself its competitors have no alternative but to follow suit, and reduce price by at least as much and possibly more in order to retain their market share. Price is now lower but with the same market share, hence the firm is on the inelastic portion of the curve ED. Price reductions may even start a price war which may be disastrous for one firm, a possibility all will want to avoid; making any reduction below P unlikely. The actual demand curve is therefore dED with prices tending to be inflexible, or rigid, around the 'kink' in the curve at E. This is one explanation of why prices tend to be inflexible in oligopolistic markets, and once firms find themselves in this situation it becomes easier to enter more formal agreements on price fixing.

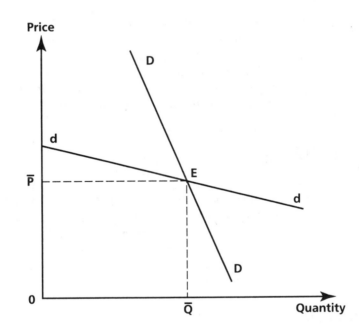

Figure 16.1

Such collusion reduces still further the risk of a price war, and in addition to price fixing may involve production quotas or other methods of reducing competition. These methods are however subject to legal controls (See Chapter 18.)

In such oligopoly situations a **price leader** may emerge. The price leader is accepted informally by all those within the industry as the firm which gives the lead in price increases. When the price leader raises the price the others take it as the signal to raise their own prices to the same level.

5 Cost differences

Even where substantial cost differences exist between two firms this may not be reflected in market prices. The 'kink' in the demand curve at E in Figure 16.2 produces a vertical section or 'discontinuity' in the marginal revenue curve of both firms, indicated by the letters G-F. Irrespective of where the firms' cost curves intersect this vertical section of the marginal revenue curve price and output will remain unchanged. In Figure 16.2 there is a low cost producer with cost curves AC' and MC' and a high cost producer with cost curves AC and MC, despite the cost differences the price for both remains P with output Q. The weakness of this analysis is that it explains **how** the kink in the demand curve occurs but cannot predict **where** it will occur and may therefore be considered as an 'ex post' rationalisation.

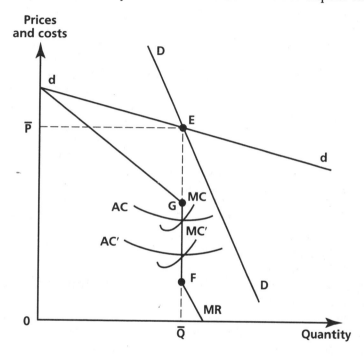

Figure 16.2

6 Non-price competition

Although firms in markets which are oligopolistic may not compete on price such markets may have the appearance of being highly competitive due to the prevalence of **non-price competition**. This non-price competition will occur because although the firms may not wish to compete on price they will still desire to increase their market share and hence their profitability. Firms will not compete on price but competition takes a variety of alternative forms.

7 Methods of non-price competition

Non-price competition may involve some, or all of the following methods:
There is usually a high level of competitive advertising. Advertising is used to

emphasise minor real, or spurious, differences between products, a process referred to as **product differentiation**; and also in the attempt to establish brand loyalty.

- 'Free' gifts.
- Competitions.
- Coupons which can be collected and exchanged for gifts.
- Special offers.
- Guarantees and warranties.
- Sponsorship.
- After sales service.

An important point is that the consumer may prefer a lower price but is not given that alternative.

8 Barriers to entry

Monopoly power, whether pure monopoly or oligopoly, will depend in the long run upon how effectively potential entrants to the industry can be kept out. Measures to keep new entrants out of an industry are referred to as **barriers to entry.** The most commonly found barriers to entry are as follows:

Extensive advertising by existing firms in order to create brand loyalty and the high level of product differentiation in the form of branded goods makes entry by new firms difficult. Initially they would at least have to match the advertising expenditure of the existing firms but on the basis of a much smaller market share.

The **minimum efficient scale (MES)** production may be high relative to the market share of the new entrant. A high MES may be due to the technical economies of scale, where for example production on a small scale is possible only at a very high cost, which on the basis of the small market share which a new entrant would have would be impossible to sustain Where the MES is low, advertising may be used as a way of increasing costs, making entry more difficult. Also where existing firms may have substantial economies of scale of the type mentioned earlier, the new entrant with a small market share will be at a considerable cost disadvantage. In addition, existing firms adopt a pricing strategy which makes entry even more difficult. In Figure 16.3 the profit maximising price for existing firms is Pe, however this is above the minimum price for a new entrant enabling them to cover their average costs and charge price Pn. Instead the existing firm may settle for a lower monopoly profit and set price at PL, below the entry price for a new entrant.

- Existing firms may have a high degree of control over the channels of distribution and may deny new entrants the means of marketing their products.
- Legal barriers may exist such as patents which hamper the entry of new firms.
- High levels of expenditure on research and development may act as a further barrier to the entry of new firms.

9 Contestable markets

The theory of contestable markets refers to oligopolistic markets where the barriers to entry are low and the threat of potential entry prevents existing oligopolists from maximising their joint profits. It is not necessary for actual entry to the market to take place

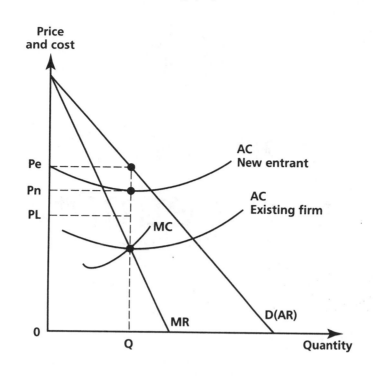

Figure 16.3

as long as the existing firms know that they face potential entry. The threat of potential entry will ensure that they set prices closer to the competitive level. Entry costs are referred to as **sunk costs**, these are the costs a firm must incur to enter a market. A market where firms can enter or leave without incurring any sunk costs is referred to as being perfectly contestable, however a market may still be perfectly contestable where sunk costs are present, provided these can be recovered following entry. Generally however the lower the sunk cost the more contestable a market is. The key points can be summarised as:

- Potential entry will modify the pricing strategies of existing firms whenever barriers to entry are low
- Firms already within the industry will take the threat of entry into account when devising their pricing and output strategies.

Self assessment questions

1 What is meant by oligopoly?
2 Explain the observed price rigidity in oligopolistic markets.
3 What is meant by non-price competition? Give examples.
4 Explain what is meant by barriers to entry.
5 What is the minimum efficient scale of an industry?
6 Discuss the theory of contestable markets in the context of barriers to entry.

17

Monopolistic competition

1 The market

Monopolistic competition is a form of imperfect competition and such markets are characterised by the prevalence of **branded goods.**

The market consists of:

- **A product group**, e.g. cigarettes, and within each product group there are:
- **Brands**, e.g. Benson & Hedges, Players, Peter Stuyvesant etc.

Each producer sells a product which is slightly different from their competitors' products and will attempt to emphasise these differences, which may be real or artificial. Where no real differences exist the producer will attempt to create them by appropriate packaging and advertising. This process of creating differences is referred to as product differentiation, and its objective is to create **brand loyalty.**

2 Monopoly power

The essential point to note is that each firm has a monopoly over its own brand because nobody else can produce it, however all the brands in the product group are in competition. The more the producer can convince consumers that their brand is different to their competitors, the stronger their market position will be.

3 Short run profits

In the short run monopoly profits will be made and the short run equilibrium position will be the same as under monopoly. This is illustrated in Figure 17.1 where the short-run equilibrium is at E with output OQ and price P, making monopoly profit POMN.

4 Barriers to entry

If the barriers to entry to the industry are weak the monopoly profits will attract new entrants into the market with similar brands. This will result in a fall in the market share of each firm. In Figure 17.2 the firm's original demand curve is DD, but as new brands enter the market it is shifted to the left to D'D'.

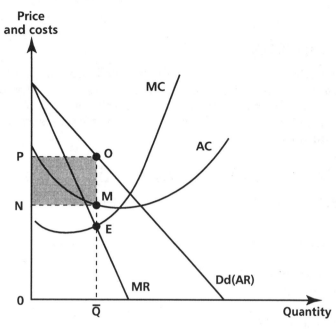

Figure 17.1

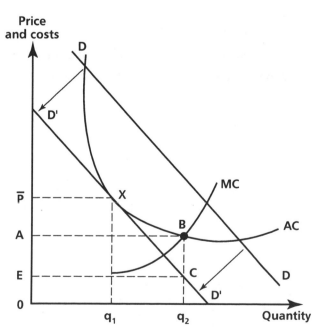

Figure 17.2

Entry to the industry will continue until all monopoly profits have been eliminated and only normal profit is being made. In Figure 17.2 this is at point X where the demand curve D'D' is tangential to the AC curve, with costs just being covered, with price $\bar{P}$ and output q_1. Losses will occur at any other output as AC will be greater than AR, for example if output is increased to q_2 a loss indicated by the area ABCE will occur, the same will be the case if output is reduced. There is therefore a long run tendency for monopoly profits to be eliminated.

5 Excess capacity

A further important characteristic which should be noted from Figure 17.2 is that the firm is not operating at the lowest point of its AC curve, it has the capacity to produce more, but cannot do so; and q_1–q_2 represents the spare capacity of the firm. As each firm is in the same situation, one of the most important long run characteristics of monopolistically competitive industries is **excess capacity.**

6 Characteristics of monopolistic competition

The characteristics of monopolistic competition are therefore:

- A wide variety of brands.
- High level of advertising and other forms of non-price competition.
- A long run tendency, in the absence of strong barriers to entry, for super normal profits to be pushed down to zero.
- Excess capacity in the industry.

Self assessment questions

1 What is a product group?

2 Explain what is meant by product differentiation.

3 Explain how monopoly profits are eliminated under conditions of monopolistic competition.

4 Why do monopolistically competitive industries suffer from excess capacity?

18

Competition policy

1 Efficiency and exploitation

Control over monopoly and restrictive practices is considered to be necessary in order to promote economic efficiency and to protect the consumer against exploitation. The economic arguments against monopoly are stated in Chapter 15, we will consider here UK legislative measures to promote competition and prevent the worst excesses of monopoly.

2 Aims of legislation

UK legislation relating to competition is directed towards:

- Dominant firm monopoly.
- Mergers which may create a monopoly position.
- Restrictive practices and resale price maintenance.

3 The UK approach

If there was a definite relationship between market structure conduct, and performance, as implied by economic theory then the solution would be to enact legislation to ban monopolies; or mergers which may result in a monopoly position. In reality however the evidence against monopolies is less clear, and in some areas gains in efficiency may outweigh the allocative costs (see Chapter 15). This has been reflected in the attitude contained within UK legislation towards monopoly and merger which is non-committal. There is no automatic assumption in law that monopoly is illegal per se (in itself) but rather is liable to case by case investigation, recognising that in some cases there may be benefits but at the same time attempting to control the abuses.

4 UK legislation

Relevant legislation, in chronological order, is as follows:

- 1948 Monopolies and Restrictive Practices Act.
- 1956 Restrictive Practices Act (Amended 1976/77)

- 1964 Resale Price Maintenance Act
- 1965 Monopolies and Mergers Act
- 1980 Competition Act

5 UK legislation in detail

The main details of the relevant legislation can be summarised as follows:

Monopolies and Restrictive Practices Act 1948. Established the Monopolies Commission to investigate cases of monopoly referred to it. Its major role was to investigate and find facts relating to cases referred to it by the Department of Trade and Industry (then Board of Trade). It was essentially powerless and could only report and not take controlling action. Monopoly was defined as control of one third of the market share.

Restrictive Trade Practices Act 1956. This act established the **Restrictive Practices Court** and a **Registrar of Restrictive Practices** to investigate agreements between firms. Such agreements covered prices and conditions of sale or supply. Restrictive practice agreements had to be registered with the Registrar and were considered to be illegal except where they could be justified through one or more of eight 'gateways' which indicated that they may be beneficial to the 'public interest'. Examples of these 'gateways' included: the agreement was protecting the public against injury, was maintaining employment or exports, made available other benefits or counteracted restrictive measures taken by another person. In a White Paper in 1989 the government proposed to strengthen this legislation by making price-fixing cartels illegal. Unfortunately a lack of Parliamentary time meant that this did not become legislation. A Green Paper in 1992, 'Abuses of Market Power' looked at the failure of existing policies to effect anti-competitive practices. This also failed to become legislation:

Resale Prices Act 1964. The practice of enforcing a retail price by a manufacturer on to a retailer was deemed to be illegal. The 1964 Act abolished the practice either collectively or individually, since the 1956 Act had still allowed the practice to continue on an individual basis. The Act allowed resale price maintenance to continue where the Restrictive Practices Court could be convinced that it would be in the 'public interest' and that abolition would cause the public to suffer in one or more of five ways, for example there would be a substantial reduction in the number of retail outlets, there would be a reduction in the quality or variety of goods available for sale or that there would be a danger to health as a consequence. Only certain drugs, books, and maps were initially exempt. Although recently the Net Book Agreement has been abolished and the Drug Agreement has been challenged.

Monopolies and Mergers Act 1965. The Act laid down that any proposed merger could be referred to the Monopolies Commission if it would result in one third of the market being controlled by a single firm or where the assets acquired exceeded £5 million (later raised to £15m).

Fair Trading Act 1973. Created the post of Director General of Fair Trading (DGFT) under whom competition and consumer law was codified and centralised. Legislation was extended to cover services such as insurance and estate agents, and the DGFT could enforce the prohibition of any practice adversely affecting consumers.

Monopolies and Mergers Act 1973. Amended the 1965 Act. The DGFT assumed responsibility for the operation of monopoly policy, and was empowered to refer monopolies to the re-named **Monopolies and Mergers Commission**. The Commission determined whether the case in question is, or is likely to be, detrimental to the public interest and to make recommendations as appropriate. Responsibility for the implementation of corrective action lies with the appropriate minister and may be by voluntary undertaking or by a binding statutory order. Monopoly was redefined as control of 25% of the market.

Competition Act 1980. The overall objective of the 1980 Act was to stimulate competition by controlling anti-competitive practices, and the legislation was extended to include the nationalised industries. The Director General was empowered to refer price issues and other specific activities to the Monopolies and Mergers Commission for investigation. Where the Commission find a practice is 'against the public interest', the Secretary of State may act to control it.. In 1981 the role of the Commission was expanded to include the efficiency of the nationalised industries. Investigations took place in 1994 into the cost of mortgage valuations and the price of compact discs and music cassettes.

6 Market concentration ratio

Monopoly legislation does not appear to have prevented the strong tendency towards market concentration in the UK. Market concentration can be expressed by means of a **market concentration ratio**. A five firm concentration ratio (CR^5) refers to the market share of the largest five firms, a two firm (CR^2) to the largest two firms, and so on, and is calculated as:

$$\text{Market concentration ratio } (CR^5) = \frac{\text{Sales of the largest 5 firms}}{\text{Total market sales}}$$

The average CR^5 rose from 55.4% in 1958 to 63.4% in 1968, and 65.1% in 1975, but declined to 42.4% in 1987, according to product group. The data also suggests a much higher level of concentration in the UK than in many comparable countries in Europe, and the USA.

7 Commission reports

The Monopolies Commission has reported on monopoly situations on a diverse range of products which has included detergents, brickmaking, brewing, breakfast cereals and solicitors services. Since 1994 criticism has been raised regarding the lack of firm remedial action by the government following publication of the Commission's reports, which have been thought to be rather timid.

Many of the reports of the Commission have criticised the restrictive practices followed by firms. For example it was critical of the practice of Roche products in charging excessively high prices to the National Health Service for the drugs Librium and Valium whilst other customers were paying much lower prices. It was also critical of Sega and Nintendo for controlling the market for video game software in 1995.

8 Restrictive agreements

Policy directed towards restrictive agreement appear to have had some degree of success. Of the 4,468 agreements which had been registered by the end of 1980, 3,295 had been disbanded and of these only 39 were as a result of a judgement by the Restrictive Practices Court, the vast majority being voluntarily disbanded. This is because a judgement applies to the whole product group and once the defence for a restrictive practice is over-ruled there is little point in anyone else proceeding. It is probable therefore that many more restrictive practices would be currently in existence in the absence of the measures taken.

9 Mergers

The control of mergers is intended to prevent monopoly situations from developing. During the 1970s there was a steady increase in the number of mergers falling within the criteria laid down by the Fair Trading Act as eligible for investigation. Since the '1965 legislation' more than 1500 mergers have been screened however of these only 53 were referred to the Monopolies and Mergers Commission, which could be taken as evidence that the official policy is not unfavourable towards mergers. Of the mergers investigated only 18 were prohibited as being against the public interest, and 18 were allowed to proceed provided certain assurances were given, the other 17 being abandoned. Whilst the trend in the 1970s and 1980s was for mergers to create even larger business units, able to compete in the Single European Market and the global markets, the fashion in the 1990s has been for demergers. This trend has been emphasised by the success and greater share values of demerged companies such as Racal/Vodaphone (formerly Racal), ICI/Zeneca (formerly ICI) and BAT/Argos/Arjo (formerly BAT Industries).

10 Office of Fair Trading

The Office of Fair Trading can only investigate those arrangements where firm evidence exists and in such cases can be said to have had a fairly high degree of success. However, many formal arrangements have probably been replaced by informal arrangements or 'gentlemen's agreements', for example trade associations circulating price lists and tacit agreements not to compete on price. Cases actually dealt with by the Restrictive Practices Court may not accurately reflect the actual extent to which such practices exist.

11 The effectiveness of legislation

The apparent ineffectiveness of monopolies and mergers legislation in the UK may reflect the flexible, or pragmatic, nature of the underlying philosophy. In particular the criteria for the investigation of mergers is quite restrictive (£ 15 million assets or 25% market share) and may not cover many mergers which do have adverse effects on competition and performance. In order to make the legislation more effective it has been suggested that an assumption should be made that certain categories of merger should be assumed to be illegal with the onus on the proposers of the merger to prove that the effects would be beneficial, others would be categorised as beneficial and allowed to proceed. A further suggestion has been that a system of fines, as is the practice in the USA should be introduced for abuses of monopoly power and that the legal system should contain a stronger presumption against monopoly.

12 Some conclusions

Competition policy in the UK can therefore be considered as relatively mild, reflecting a flexible attitude towards monopoly with no automatic assumption against any particular monopoly or merger, each case being treated on its merits. Legislation has therefore probably done little other than to remove the worst and most visible restrictive practices and abuses of monopoly power.

Dissatisfaction with existing restrictive practices legislation has resulted in the publication of a White Paper (Opening Markets: New Policy on Restrictive Trade Practices, July 1989, Cm 727) which contained new proposals for the control of restrictive practices to be introduced during 1990. The new proposals represented a fundamental change of emphasis from the previous rules. Agreements and practices with anti-competitive effects were to be prohibited outright instead of being made subject to a requirement to register. The system of registering agreements was to be scrapped and instead time and resources were to be concentrated on dealing with agreements which did raise competition problems. Also UK law was to be made compatible with European Community law and the legislation was to be extended to include the professional bodies which were previously excluded. Under the proposed legislation the DGFT was to investigate cases arising and publish conclusions on them. Under the proposals a new Restrictive Trade Practices tribunal was to be established to reach decisions when those of the DGFT were disputed, to impose penalties on firms where warranted, and to consult with the DGFT when recommending exemptions.

Unfortunately these proposals never became legislation.

Self assessment questions

1 Why is it considered necessary to have legislation for the control of monopolies and mergers?

2 Explain what is meant by the term 'restrictive practices'.

3 What is the attitude towards monopolies and mergers which is reflected in UK legislation?

4 What is meant by a five firm concentration ratio?

5 How effective do you consider competition policy in the UK to have been?

19

Wages

1 Rewards to labour

Wages are the payments received in return for labour services and as such are the returns received by **labour** as a factor of production.

2 Wage rates

It is necessary however to explain why it is that the **wage rates** differ between occupations. In order to explain these wage differentials it is necessary to consider both demand and supply in the labour market.

3 Marginal productivity theory of wages

One explanation is the **marginal productivity theory of wages**. The law of declining marginal productivity was explained in Chapter 2. It will be recalled that the marginal product (MP) is the addition to total output or product which occurs when one additional unit of a variable factor is added to a fixed factor. It will be recalled that MP initially rises but then starts to decline as diminishing returns set in. Total product rises but at a declining rate. In this particular case the variable factor is labour and all other factors are fixed. The theory also makes a number of other assumptions:

- Conditions of perfect competition, therefore the firm can obtain all the labour it requires at the prevailing wage rate.
- Labour is an homogeneous factor, i.e. the productivity of each unit of labour is the same.
- Perfect mobility of labour between occupations.
- The entrepreneur's aim is to maximise profits, therefore the main concern will be the difference between the cost of employing labour and the revenue to be gained from the sale of the output of labour.

4 Marginal Revenue Product

Marginal revenue product (MRP) refers to the addition to total revenue received from the sale of the additional unit of output, and is calculated as the marginal physical product (MPP), e.g. tonnes of potatoes etc., multiplied by price, i.e. MPP × P = MRP.

As under conditions of perfect competition price is constant the MPP curve will be identical in shape to the MRP curve. Under conditions of imperfect competition the MRP curve is obtained by multiplying the MPP by marginal revenue, i.e. MPP × MR = MRP. Note that as P = MR under perfect competition, then as a general rule MPP × MR = MRP in both perfect and imperfect competition.

5 MRP and ARP curves

In Figure 20.1 the MRP curve can be seen to rise and then fall cutting the average revenue product (ARP) curve at its highest point. The ARP curve represents the average return, in monetary terms, per unit of labour employed. As a result of the competitive assumption the supply of labour will be perfectly elastic at the prevailing wage rate, W^0, which is determined by the **market**. Recalling the assumption of profit maximisation it is evident that the entrepreneur will want to employ labour as long as the MRP is greater than the wage rate (cost of labour) in Figure 19.1 he will continue to employ additional labour up to $O\bar{Q}$ his will add more to revenue than to costs. Above $O\bar{Q}$ additional labour will cost more than its MRP and will not therefore be employed. The profit maximising entrepreneur will therefore employ $O\bar{Q}$ labour. If we consider the wage rate the marginal cost of labour we can see that the conclusion is another form of the MR = MC rule encountered under the theory of the firm, point E being the equilibrium point.

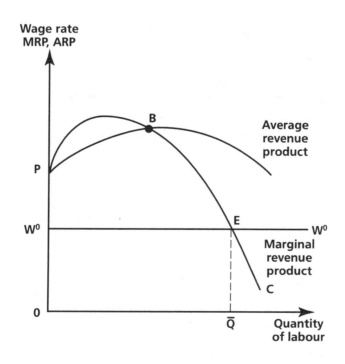

Figure 19.1

6 The demand for labour

The relevant section of the MRP curve is however B–C only. This is because no firm would employ labour when the wage rate is greater than the ARP as the profit maximising entrepreneur would never pay more to all workers than the highest ARP, as losses would result. The section of the MRP curve below ARP, i.e. B–C can be considered as the competitive firm's **demand curve for labour.**

MRP theory is therefore a theory of how the **demand** for labour is determined, but as the supply of labour is excluded it cannot be considered as a theory of how wages are determined as it says nothing about the determination of wage rates.

7 MRP theory

MRP theory however can be useful as a tool for analysing the effects on the demand for labour of the changes in the relevant variables. In Figure 19.2 an increase in the wage rate from W^0 to W^1 will result in a reduction in the quantity of labour employed from Q^0 to Q'. If however the MRP curve can be shifted upwards and outwards from MRP' to MRP'' then the quantity of labour can remain unchanged at Q^0.

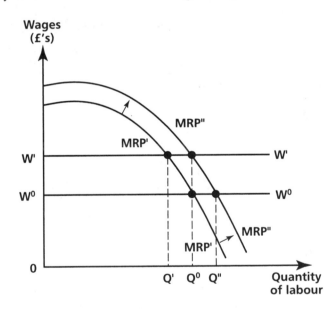

Figure 19.2

Alternatively if the shift in the MRP curve takes place with the wage rate remaining constant at W^0 the amount of labour employed would increase to Q'' or the existing work force Q^0 could enjoy the higher wage rate. Shifts in the MRP curve from MRP' to MRP'' can be brought about by:

- An increase in productivity brought about by the abandonment of a previously held restrictive practice.
- The adoption of new technology which makes labour more productive.
- An increase in the price of the product – which may be difficult given the competitive assumption.

8 Labour demand characteristics

The demand for labour has four characteristics which affect the extent to which the labour force can affect the wage rate.

- The demand for labour is a **derived demand**, i.e. The demand for labour is derived from the product it produces, the greater the demand for the product the greater the demand for labour.
- The elasticity of demand for labour is derived from the elasticity of demand for the product; the greater the elasticity of demand for the product the greater the elasticity of demand for the labour producing it.
- The proportion of total cost accounted for by labour – the lower this is the more scope labour will have to gain increases in wages.
- The extent to which capital can be substituted for labour in the production process, the easier this is the weaker will be the position of labour.

9 The labour market

The wage rate in a particular occupation is determined by the interaction of demand and supply in that particular labour market. The labour market is not a single homogeneous market but consists of thousands of different markets each with its own particular supply curve. The elasticity of the labour supply curve will depend upon factors such as the amount of training and skill required and the duration of the training period required. The supply curve may be more inelastic due to restrictions upon entry to an occupation, where for example, trade unions insist upon lengthy apprenticeships. Figure 19.3 represents the supply curve for a relatively unskilled occupation where an increase in the wage rate from W' to W'' leads to a more than proportionate increase in the supply of labour from Q' to Q''.

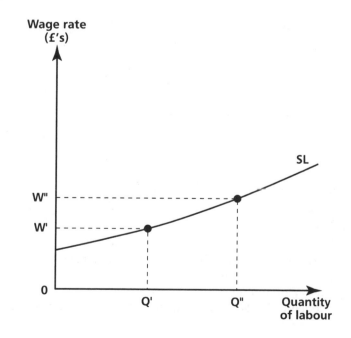

Figure 19.3

The same magnitude of increase in the skilled occupation, represented in Figure 19.4, has a far less significant effect upon the supply of labour, Q' to Q'' due to the training period required to acquire the necessary skills, or restrictions placed upon entry.

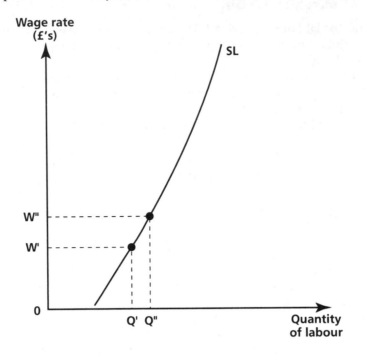

Figure 19.4

10 Wage theory omissions

Other points for consideration which wage theory does not incorporate, but may affect wages, include:

- Legislation such as the Sex Discrimination and Equal Pay Acts 1975.
- Incomes policies, under which governments have attempted to control the rate of wage increase according to some predetermined 'norm'.
- Government management of the economy and the effects of inflationary/deflationary measures, and tax policy.

11 The bargaining theory of wages

The bargaining theory of wages views wages as being the outcome of negotiations between two powerful monopoly groups, on the one hand the trade unions who monopolise the supply of labour, and on the other the employers' organisations who monopolise the demand. The relative bargaining strengths of the two parties will vary between different time periods according to changes in the economic climate. For example, during recession the employers will be in the stronger bargaining position and during economic boom when the demand for labour is high, the trade unions will be in a stronger position.

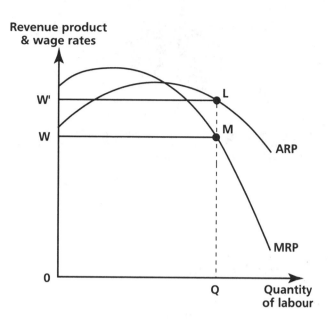

Figure 19.5

Bargaining theory can however be incorporated within marginal productivity theory. In Figure 19.5 the current wage rate is OW, and recalling that the entrepreneur will never pay a wage greater than the ARP of labour, we can see that the highest wage which would be paid is OW' (QL). LM is the surplus earned by the entrepreneur on each worker employed (OQ). A wage increase above OW would normally reduce the quantity of labour employed. If however the workforce is strongly unionised they may be able to resist the reduction in the workforce and persuade the employer to pay the increase out of the surplus L–M. The extent to which L–M will be shared with the workforce depends upon relative bargaining strengths at the time.

12 Some conclusions

Despite the criticisms of marginal productivity theory the principles it contains appear to be inescapable in the long run and it does appear that any wage increases which are considerably above the rate of productivity increase will result in a reduction in the size of the work force. Marginal productivity is therefore probably always present at the bargaining table, whether the parties to the bargain are aware of it or not; but there are so many other factors influencing wages that it is probably not a fully adequate explanation of any particular wage rate.

Self assessment questions

1 Which section of the MRP curve represents the firm's demand curve for labour?
2 How does the competitive firm decide how much labour to employ?
3 State the weaknesses of MRP theory as a theory of wage determination.
4 Outline an alternative theory of wage determination.
5 Discuss the factors other than MRP which may influence wages.
6 How relevant is marginal productivity theory in a modern economy?

20

Trade unions

1 The role of trade unions

The economic theory of wage determination is discussed in Chapter 19, however it is impossible in an industrial society to analyse the factors which determine wages without giving some consideration to the role and influence of **trade unions.**

Although we are mainly concerned here with the affect of trade unions on wages, it is important to be aware of the wider role of trade unions. The Donovan Report (1968) considered the role of trade unions under three main headings:

- Promoting the interests of their members.
- Accelerating the economic advance of the nation.
- Accelerating the social advance of the nation.

2 Collective bargaining

Wage rates and conditions are determined by the process referred to as **collective bargaining,** whereby the union officials bargain with employers on behalf of their members.

Collective bargaining generally occurs at the national level and the pay rates determined apply to a whole industry and are embodied within a national agreement. This agreement may be supplemented by additional payments or benefits negotiated locally at plant level. Nationwide collective bargaining has the advantage for both unions and management of reducing the costs of bargaining below what it would be if employers and employees negotiated individually.

3 Membership

Trade union membership in the UK grew throughout the 20th century, but with the main periods of growth being around the two World Wars, the late 1960s and the 1970s; but with membership declining in the 1980s and 1990s as a consequence of rising unemployment and government legislation. Table 20.1 indicates the pattern of trade union membership in the UK.

TABLE 20.1				
Year	Men	Women (millions)	Total	Total membership as a % of total employees
1951	7.7	1.8	9.5	45
1961	7.9	2.0	9.9	43
1971	8.4	2.8	11.1	49
1981	8.4	3.8	12.1	50
1986	6.8	3.7	10.5	44
1990	5.3	3.5	8.8	38
1991	5.1	3.5	8.6	37
1992	4.6	3.4	8.0	36
1993	4.4	3.4	7.8	35
1994	4.2	3.3	7.5	34
1995	4.1	3.2	7.3	32

4 Raising wage rates

It is often argued that unions can raise their members' wage rates only at the cost of reducing the number employed. Such analysis assumes that the demand for labour is competitive and the demand curve is static. In Figure 20.1, DD is the demand curve for labour and SS the supply curve.

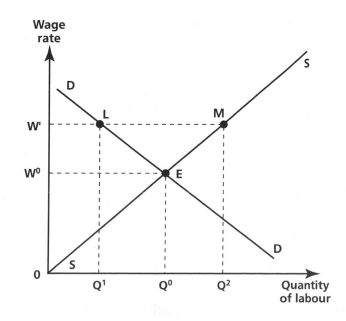

Figure 20.1

The equilibrium wage is W^0 with Q^0 labour employed. If the union now enforces a wage increase to W^1 which is the minimum wage at which union members are allowed to work, the demand for labour falls to Q^1 (L) as a consequence of:

- The higher price being charged for the product being produced, which is necessary to cover the wage rise.
- Factor substitution as capital is substituted for labour in the production process as it is now relatively cheaper.

The supply curve for labour is now W^1 M S with no labour supplied below the minimum wage (W^1) and an infinite amount up to $M(Q^2)$, the labour supply curve is therefore infinitely elastic along the portion W^1 L M, but the labour supply will not increase above $M(Q^2)$ without a higher wage rate. The new supply curve intersects the original demand curve at L, the new equilibrium point, with Q^1 labour demanded, whilst the quantity supplied at that wage rate is Q^2. The quantity of labour employed has been reduced by $Q^0 - Q^1$ and there is an excess labour supply of $Q^1 - Q^2$ (L–M) at the prevailing wage rate. This type of analysis however ignores changes in productivity and Chapter 19 shows how an **increase in the marginal productivity of labour can maintain the numbers employed.** Such increases in marginal productivity can be achieved through the adoption of new technology and more efficient working practices.

5 Trade union influence

The extent to which a union can influence wages in a particular industry also depends upon the elasticity of demand for labour. (This is discussed in Chapter 19).

Generally it is the case that the more inelastic the demand for labour the greater the scope a union will have for gaining a wage increase for its members. In any particular occupation the scope for gaining wage increases will also be influenced by supply factors, the more inelastic the supply the greater the scope for maintaining, or obtaining, high wage rates. Unions therefore have an incentive to restrict the supply of labour to any particular occupation by imposing entry conditions such as lengthy apprenticeships. Where there are few restrictions upon entry to an occupation, i.e. unskilled occupations, the union may need to substitute the threat of withdrawal of labour as a means of influencing wages.

The extent to which unions can raise the wage rates of their members may also depend upon a number of other factors such as the attitudes of the membership, the degree of geographical concentration, the stability of employment, and the degree of competition amongst employers. Studies, in the late 1980s, indicate that the hourly pay rate in an industry where the labour force was unionised and covered by a collective bargaining agreement was 8–10% higher than in a similar non-unionised industry. However in the 1990s the reduction in the power of the unions has in return reduced this differential.

6 Pay differentials

Trade unions, and relative demand elasticities are important factors in explaining the pay differentials which exist between occupations, a particularly important source of higher earnings being the length of training and level of education required. Adam Smith referred to **equalizing** and **non-equalizing** differentials and suggested that in a competitive labour market the **net advantages** of an occupation would **tend to equality**.

Equalising advantages were factors such as unpleasantness, dirt and discomfort, non-equalising differentials were wages. In an unpleasant occupation there would be higher wages to compensate and in pleasant occupations wages would be lower, and over a lifetime the net advantages between occupations will be equalised. In reality it is frequently the lowest paid occupations which are also the most unpleasant, as they are generally unskilled, entry to them is easy, and those in such occupations have no alternative available to them.

7 Factors creating wage differentials

Wages may also differ between people in the same occupations. One reason may be differentials as a reward for experience or length of service, or where pay scales are structured according to age. A major source of wage differentials is sex, as women even within the same occupation are frequently paid less than men. Women also tend to be concentrated into the occupations with the lowest rates of pay, such as catering and hairdressing. The combination of these factors means that on average women earn considerably less than men, and studies suggest that women's earnings are approximately 75% of men's despite the Equal Pay Act 1975. The main reasons suggested for this apparent discrimination against women are:

- Their weaker attachment to the labour force due to the convention that they look after children, and the need to be absent from work when having children.
- Absenteeism and labour turnover is higher for women than it is for men.
- As a consequence of the weaker attachment to the labour force women gain less experience and seniority in the work-place, and employers are less willing therefore to give training to women, which reduces their value in the workforce.
- Women tend to be concentrated in industries which consist of numerous small-scale establishments in which national wage rates tend to be lower than in the larger more concentrated industries. These also tend to be industries in which a lower proportion of the workforce belongs to trade unions due to the high costs of organising.
- Even within the same occupational group, women tend to earn less than men, for example, within primary school teaching women earn approximately 12% less than men, although the main source of this differential is not that women are paid less for the same job but that fewer of them occupy the higher paid teaching positions, due probably to the reasons given above.

If it is also considered that females work predominately part-time, (40% of total females in work compared to 5% for males) then the disparity in wages becomes even more pronounced. The anomaly of low pay for women has been only marginally influenced by Equal Pay legislation, despite the fact that this legislation together with the Sex Discrimination Act (1975) and the Employment Protection Act (1976) are now over 20 years old. If however, for the reasons given above, it is not discrimination but a reflection of a lower marginal revenue product which results in lower female wages then it may also be necessary to raise the marginal productivity of women by giving them more incentive to remain in the workforce; for example, better career prospects, training and a more appropriate educational structure.

8 Trade union reforms

The 1980s saw the largest programme of trade union reform ever. The motives were part-ly political but also to reduce the influence of the unions on the labour market (see Chapter 19). Many of these reforms were consolidated in the 1992 Act of Parliament and further measures were taken in the 1993 Act. The reforms have included the following measures;

- Trade unions must conduct a secret postal ballot before they can approve industrial action
- it is illegal to enforce closed shops
- picketing must be peaceful and is limited to the employees place of work
- union subscriptions can only be deducted from an employees wage after permission has been given. This process must be repeated every three years
- the abolition of the Wages Council
- Union officials must be elected every 5 years

The result of these measures, and others not listed, has been a weakening of the unions bargaining position and, some believe, a reason for the reduction of their membership. Figure 20.2 illustrates the decline in trade union membership between 1979 and 1995.

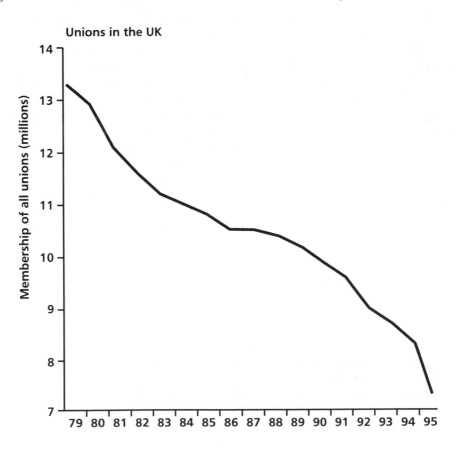

Figure 20.2

Self assessment questions

1 What is meant by 'collective bargaining'?

2 Under what circumstances can a trade union simultaneously raise wages and maintain employment?

3 Explain the differences in wage rates both between occupations and between males and females.

4 What is meant by equalising and non-equalising differentials?

5 Account for the decline in trade union membership in the 1980s and 1990s.

21

Rent

1 A definition

Rent in everyday terms refers to a regular payment made in return for the use of an asset, in economics however the term has a far more specific meaning. In economics rent refers to the **payment to a factor of production which is in fixed supply.**

2 Economic rent

The concept of economic rent was originally applied to land only. **David Ricardo** was one of the earliest economists to discuss the theory. Ricardo noted that as the supply of land was fixed, with no way of increasing or decreasing it, supply could not respond to changes in demand. If this was the case, what then determined the price of the land? The 'supply price' refers to the minimum payment which is necessary to keep a factor of production in its current use, and as the supply of land cannot be varied, it has no supply price. Any payment to a factor of production which is above the supply price is a surplus, and is referred to as **economic rent. Rent therefore is any surplus above the supply price.** As land is perfectly inelastic in supply, and therefore has no supply price, the whole of the return to the landlord for land is economic rent, i.e.

economic rent = current earnings – supply price

During the Napoleonic Wars grain prices rose to very high levels and many people blamed this on the high price, and therefore rents, of agricultural land. Ricardo however pointed out the flaw in this explanation. As the supply of land was fixed and therefore could not vary with demand, the price of land could not determine grain prices. The only demand for land is in fact a **derived demand**, derived from the demand for grain. If the demand for grain is high the price is high, which enables the landlord to charge a higher rent for grain growing land. Should the demand for grain fall however, the landlord would be forced to take whatever rent could be obtained as the land would still be there even if the return was zero. In reality of course land has alternative uses and at some point it may be more profitable to transfer it to some alternative use such as potatoes.

3 Pure economic rent

Figure 21.1 illustrates the concept of pure economic rent. The supply of the factor of production is fixed at $O\bar{Q}$ with demand DD and price P^0, the shaded area $OP^0E\bar{Q}$ economic rent. An increase in the demand for the factor to D'D' increases the rent by $P^0P^1E^1E$. As the supply has remained unchanged at $O\bar{Q}$ all of the additional factor income is rent.

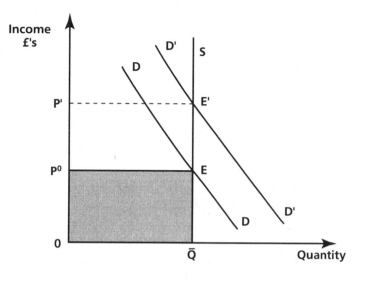

Figure 21.1

4 Rent of ability

Figure 21.1 could be used to illustrate the supply of individuals with unique talents, for example, certain entertainers, footballers and other sportsmen, great actors or skilful entrepreneurs. Such talents earn what is referred to as **rent of ability.**

5 Quasi-rent

When a factor is in temporarily fixed supply, for example a class of skilled labour, and economic rents will be earned in the short-run only, in this case until more people can be trained; then the rent is referred to as **quasi-rent.**

6 Transfer earnings

Although the amount of land, or any other factor, may be fixed, in reality it is unlikely to be specific to a single use only and may be transferred to alternative uses. For example, agricultural land may be used as building land, or transferred to alternative agricultural uses. The minimum payment which is necessary to retain a factor of production in its current use and prevent it from transferring to its next best alternative is known as its **transfer earnings**. Transfer earnings can be considered as the opportunity cost of keeping a factor in its current use. Where a factor has alternative uses **any payment made over** the factor's transfer earnings is economic rent. For example, a footballer earning £2,500 per week who has also trained as a plumber, and could earn £ 250 per week at plumbing. If his earnings as a footballer began to fall he would transfer to plumbing when his wages as a footballer fell below £250.

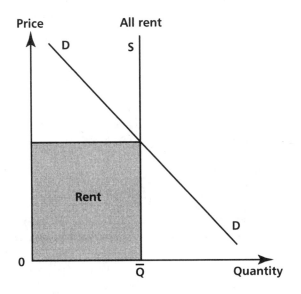

Figure 21.2

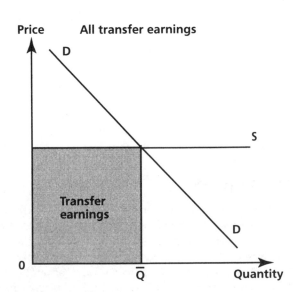

Figure 21.3

7 The importance of elasticity

Wherever a factor of production has an upward sloping supply curve, part of its earnings will be rent and part transfer earnings. The proportions of rent and transfer earnings depend upon the elasticity of supply of the factor. The less elastic is the supply the greater the proportion of economic rent, the greater the elasticity of supply the greater are the transfer earnings. In the extreme case of zero elasticity of supply, all the return is rent and where elasticity of supply is infinity it is all transfer earnings. The extreme case of all rent is illustrated in Figure 21.2, and all transfer earnings in Figure 21.3. In Figure 21.4 the factor earnings are equally divided between rent and transfer earnings.

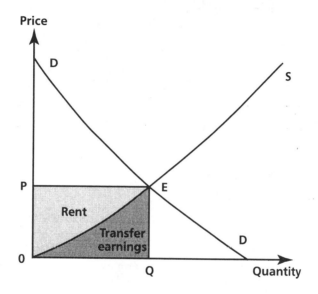

Figure 21.4

8 Alternative uses

City centre land sites are extremely expensive, which is a consequence of the highly inelastic supply. The supply of such sites is extremely restricted and each site has many competing uses. Demand is continually rising but the supply of sites for cinemas, restaurants, car parks, offices and shops cannot be increased. The high price of such sites results from the increasing demand and inelastic supply, however as the sites have many alternative uses the element of rent in the price for any particular use will be quite small, the greatest element being transfer earnings. The earnings in any particular use will have to be at least sufficient to prevent it from transferring to the next best alternative, for example, the high price of cinema tickets in city centres reflects the need for cinemas to earn sufficient returns to prevent them from being transferred to use as restaurants or offices. In Figure 21.5 demand curve DD represents the demand for an urban site for use as a restaurant, for which the price would be P^0 and D'D' the demand for the same site as a cinema, for which the market price which people are willing to pay is P^1. Only the shaded area $P^0P^1E^1E$, the surplus over the next best alternative use, is economic rent.

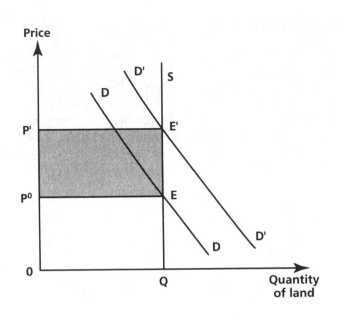

Figure 22.5

9 Economic rent a tax

It has been suggested in the past that the economic rents earned on land should be the basis for taxation. This suggestion is generally associated with Henry George, who advocated the use of such a tax in the USA during the 19th century. The land tax was to be the single source of taxation and was justified on the grounds that as the supply of land is fixed, the returns to the owner may rise without any extra effort on his behalf. It was this 'unearned increment' upon which the tax was to be levied, and as the supply of land was fixed the tax could not be avoided (i.e. the 'tax base' could not be eroded). The proposal to tax the economic rent on land has two main difficulties:

- How to distinguish between rent and transfer earnings.
- The problem of identifying the element of rent, recalling that the amount of commercial rent paid to the landlord is not the same as economic rent.

Similar arguments to those used in favour of the land tax have been used in support of the arguments to tax the rent element in the earnings of individuals with unique talents such as musicians, entertainers and footballers.

10 Essential points

The essential points to bear in mind are:

- rents do not determine prices, it is prices which determine rents.
- rent is a surplus which becomes greater as the price of the product from which the demand for the factor is derived increases.

Self assessment questions

1 Distinguish between economic rent and rent in its everyday context.
2 Outline the factors which determine economic rent.
3 Distinguish between rent and transfer earnings.
4 What is meant by quasi-rent?
5 Why are house prices in city centres higher than elsewhere?

22

Population

1 Introduction

Population refers to the number of people living in a particular area. In the study of population however, it is not only the absolute number of people which is of interest, but also the rate of change of the population size and also its composition. The study of population is important because of its economic implications, in particular the way in which change in the population can affect changes in the demand for goods and services, and therefore the allocation of society's resources.

2 Population growth

The total population of the UK, and the rest of the world, was characterised by a rapid growth throughout the 19th century and this growth has continued in the rest of the world throughout the 20th century, although in the UK since 1971 the total has remained fairly level with only slow growth projected to the end of the century. Table 22.1 shows the population growth for the UK. The size of the UK population is found from a census which has been held every 10 years since 1801.

3 Population composition

Although it is important to know the size of the total population it is also important to have details of the composition of the population, in particular an estimate is required of the following.

- **Working population –** the proportion of the population in the working age group 16 –65 (60 for females).
- **Age/sex structure –** Age structure refers to the number of persons in each of three groupings. (i) Young persons – below 16. (ii) Working age groups, 16–65. (iii) Men and women over 65.

Age/sex distribution refers to the number of males and females in each age grouping.

TABLE 22.1 UK population (millions)	
1851	22.3
1901	38.2
1921	44.0
1931	46.0
1951	50.2
1961	52.7
1971	55.5
1981	56.3
1991	57.6
1995	58.9
2001	(forecast) 59.8
2011	(forecast) 61.4

4 Standard of living

Both total population and the population structure have important implications for the nation's standard of living. Income per head or **per capita income** for a nation is calculated as:

$$\text{per capita income} = \frac{\text{national income}}{\text{population}}$$

From this equation it can be seen that even if national income is growing per capita income may fall if the rate of growth of national income is exceeded by the rate of growth of population, and it is this problem which faces many 'third world' countries.

5 Changes in the composition

Changes in the composition of the population alters the balance between producers and consumers over time. As stated above the age group 16–65 form the working population whilst those in the 0–16 and 65+ groups can be regarded as the dependent population.. An increase in the size of the dependent population relative to the working population, referred to as the dependency ratio, means that living standards would fall unless there is an increase in the real output of the working population as a result of increased productivity, for example; by the adoption of new technology. Changes in the composition of the population also affects the demand for age related goods and services, and for this reason has important implications for firms, local authorities and central government. An increase in the proportion of people in the 65+ age group, referred to as an ageing population, increases the demand for social provision for the aged, appropriate medical provision, and increases the burden of pensions on the working population. Although the UK population remained fairly level between 1971 and 1991 the proportion aged less than 16 fell and the proportion over 65 increased. Population projections up to 2011 show a rise in the numbers over 65 with the most significant increase in those over 85. Within the older age group females predominate as their life expectancy exceeds that of males. In 1994 women outnumbered men in the age group of 65 upwards, and in the 80 or over age group the ratio of women to men was over 2 to 1. Both females and males today however have a 50% chance of achieving a life expectancy of 70 years. This increase in life expectancy has been the result of the improvement in living standards, medical advances, and the extension of welfare services for the older age groups.

6 Population pyramids

The age/sex distribution of the population can be illustrated by the use of population pyramids as shown in Figure 22.1

The population pyramid illustrates the age/sex distribution of the population, the dotted lines showing the affect of an ageing population on the shape of the population pyramid.

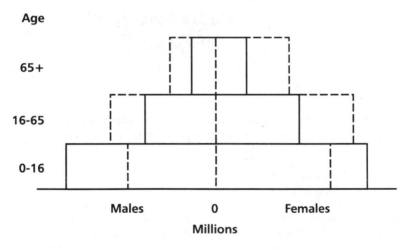

Figure 22.1

7 Birth and death rates

Births and deaths are usually expressed as crude birth and death rates. These are calculated as the number of births/deaths per 1000 population.

$$\frac{\textbf{number of births} \times \textbf{1000}}{\textbf{total population}}$$

The crude birth rate is influenced by factors such as the state of medical knowledge, social and economic factors, social mores such as the attitudes towards family size, contraception, and religion.

The crude death rate is influenced by social and economic conditions, medical knowledge, hygiene and living standards, and the infant mortality rate (ie. the deaths of children below 1 year of age).

8 Life expectancy

The improvement in the average life expectancy in the UK to 70 years has been the result of the advances in medical care and the extension of welfare services for the elderly and in addition the affect of the general rise in living standards. The most significant fall in the death rate has resulted from lower infant mortality which has been a consequence of improved medical facilities, improvements in diet and housing, and the improvements in ante and post natal care.

9 Changes in population size

The overall size of the population is determined by the natural increase, ie. births minus deaths. In the UK during the 20th century the change in the birth rate is seen as being the major influence on population size as the death rate has remained fairly constant. The birth rate, despite its falling trend, is more liable to sudden variations. Unexpected increases in the birth rate, or 'baby booms', create population bulges such as those which occurred after the two World Wars and in the mid-1960s. Such bulges then pass through the population structure over time, creating an increased demand for age related goods and services which may not be required in such quantities when the bulge in the population has passed. For example, the 'baby booms' of the mid-1960s increased the demand for schools, but as the bulge passed into the older age group the demand for schooling fell resulting in falling school rolls and surplus school capacity. In the 21st century there will be an increase in the demand for pensions as the population bulge moves into the pensionable age group.

The major changes in population are of three types:

- **birth rate exceeding death rate** resulting in an **increasing population**.
- **death rate exceeding birth rate** resulting in a **decreasing population**.
- **exceptional increases** in the birth rate resulting in a **population bulge**.

Net migration which is calculated as **immigration minus emigration** has not seriously affected the UK population over the long term. Net migration is more likely to affect the quality of the working population, particularly if the most talented, healthiest, or skilled members of the workforce choose to emigrate.

10 Optimum population

The concept of the optimum population is central to the study of the economics of population. Optimum population can be defined as the population size which maximises the output (per head) of the economy. The concept of optimum population assumes that technology, trade and competition remains constant and only the population size varies. Given these assumptions, then as the population size increases output will initially increase, but eventually diminishing returns set in and as population grows further output per head declines. This is illustrated in Figure 22.2. Output per head is maximised at X with population OM.

Increases in population above OM cause output per head to fall and M–R can therefore be referred to as over-populated, with population OR giving a lower per capital income (OC) than population OM. Population ON fails to exploit the returns to scale and therefore also has a lower per capita income than OM; also having per capita income OC. ON can therefore be referred to as being under-populated.

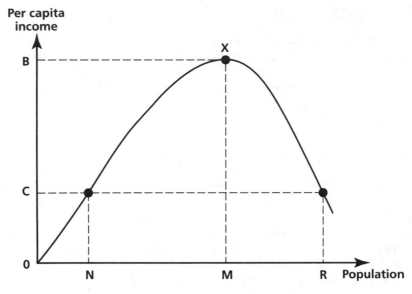

Figure 22.2

If the assumption that technology is fixed is dropped however, it may be possible for increased productivity through technological change to offset the effect of diminishing returns and the optimum population may coincide with the actual population as population grows. In Figure 22.3 as population grows from OM to OT technological change increases productivity per head offsetting the effect of diminishing returns shifting the most efficient, or optimum, point from X to S; the optimum population being the same as the actual population OT.

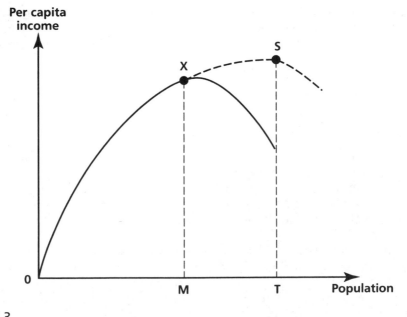

Figure 22.3

As population growth takes place, there could be a succession of points such as X and S each giving a higher per capita income and therefore standard of living.

11 Rev. Thomas Malthus – Essay on population

One of the earliest discussions of population size was that by the Rev. Thomas Malthus in his essay 'The Principle of Population as it affects the future improvement of Society' (1798), which was refined in a second essay in 1803. Malthus examined the relationship between population size and the means of subsistence; in particular the production of food. Malthus postulated that any increase in living standards would result in an increase in population size, however food production could not increase at the same rate as population growth. Population growth would therefore always exceed the growth of the means of subsistence and mankind was doomed to remain in poverty living at the subsistence level. According to Malthus the population was kept within its means of subsistence by the 'misery' of famine, war, disease, and pestilence. The only escape for civilisation from this vicious circle of poverty was through what Malthus referred to as 'moral restraint' by which he meant later marriage and therefore fewer children—a solution Malthus himself thought was unlikely.

Malthus' gloomy predictions proved to be incorrect—the population during the 19th century grew rapidly and so too did living standards. The weaknesses in Malthus' argument were as follows:

- The Malthusian argument is essentially one of diminishing returns with land as a fixed factor. In fact land was not a fixed factor as new food growing areas were developed overseas and food was imported, eg. wheat from the American prairies.
- Malthus did not foresee the rate of technological change which enabled living standards to rise alongside population growth.
- Improvements in methods of birth control and their general acceptance within society, and changed social attitudes towards family size.
- Malthus considered people only as consumers but generally each consumer is also a producer, therefore a larger population creates a greater output.

12 Neo – Malthusianism

The Malthusian doctrine can therefore be considered as a special case of the law of diminishing returns, the affects of which were offset in Britain by changes in other factors as listed above. The lessons of Malthus cannot however be totally ignored as it will always be necessary to relate finite resources to the demands of society and in many 'third world' countries where populations are growing more rapidly than the means of subsistence the principles advocated by Malthus are still relevant today. The application of Malthusian principles to the world situation is sometimes referred to as neo-Malthusianism.

Self assessment questions

1 What are the main causes of changes in the population size?

2 What is meant by the term 'optimum population'?

3 How does a change in the population structure affect the demand for goods and services?

4 What did Malthus predict about the future of mankind and why was he proved wrong?

23

Interest

1 Factor reward

Interest is the factor reward, or earnings, of **capital**. Alternatively it can be considered as the payment for the use of money. This money may be used for the purchase of capital equipment, but may also be used for alternative purposes. This source of finance will only be available if other people are willing to forego consumption and provide a pool of financial resources from which loans can be made. This supply of funds will only be forthcoming if those supplying the funds receive some reward for sacrificing their current consumption and are compensated for the risks involved; in particular the

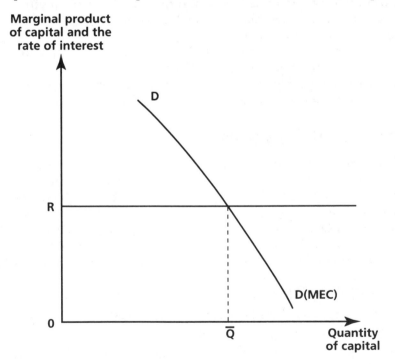

Figure 23.1

possibility of not getting their money back, or the possibility of a reduction in the value of their money due to inflation. Interest can therefore be considered as the price of borrowing money.

2 The demand for capital

The **demand for capital** can be analysed in a manner which is almost identical to the marginal productivity of labour theory of wages.

If the stock of capital is increased relative to other factors of production, diminishing returns will eventually set in as capital, like the other factors of production, is subject to the law of diminishing marginal productivity. The **marginal productivity of capital curve (MP)** in Figure 23.1 represents the firm's demand for capital curve. This is known also as the **marginal efficiency of capital curve (MEC)**. It slopes downwards due to diminishing returns and as the rate of interest is the cost of capital the capital stock will be expanded to just the point at which the cost is equal to the value of the marginal product. The firm will therefore employ $O\overline{Q}$ capital at interest rate R. Profitability is therefore maximised when: **mp of capital = rate of interest**.

As was the case in the analysis of wages, a change in either the physical productivity of capital or in the price of goods produced will bring about a shift in the MP curve and therefore the demand for capital.

Analysis is in fact more complicated than this as investment decisions are taken on the basis of anticipated returns from the investment over the lifetime of the capital compared with the current outlay. This approach requires the use of discounting to obtain the 'present value' of the investment's yield.

3 Classical theory

If the rate of interest is the 'price' of borrowed funds, then if we wish to formulate a theory of how interest rates are determined, we must also consider the supply of funds for lending. The theory that the interest rate is determined by the demand and supply for loanable funds is referred to as the **classical theory** of interest rate determination.

The supply of loanable funds for investment is determined by current savings. The supply curve in Figure 23.2 is society's savings function, the shape of which represents the **time preference** of individuals, i.e. the extent to which present consumption is preferred to future consumption. A rate of interest is necessary to compensate savers for the loss of current purchasing power, and is therefore necessary in order to induce savings. The intersection of the demand and supply curves gives the equilibrium rate of interest. If desired saving is greater than the demand for investment purposes there will be an excess supply of savings which will push down the rate of interest until equilibrium between demand and supply is re-established. If demand exceeds supply the rate of interest will rise until sufficient extra savings are forthcoming to re-establish an equilibrium.

- Classical theory is referred to as a 'flow theory' because it assumes that a continuous flow of savings is possible at the prevailing rate of interest.
- According to classical theory, savings are not assumed to be a function of (dependent upon) the level of income.

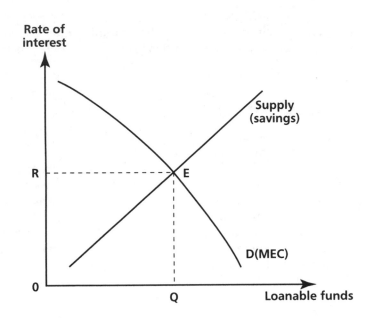

Figure 23.2

4 Determinants of saving

The major determinants of saving are as follows:

- The level of income. As incomes rise the proportion of income devoted to consumption tends to decline, hence in economies where incomes are high the proportion of saving tends to be higher.
- The extent to which the financial structure of the economy has developed thereby providing a range of institutions where savings can be safely deposited and where they can earn an adequate return with a minimum of risk.
- The extent to which a society views thrift as being a virtue or otherwise. This can vary between different societies, or within the same society over different time periods. In Victorian times thrift was seen as being far more virtuous than it is in the present day.

5 Types of savings

Savings can be of several different types.

- Personal savings consist of the money which households choose not to spend from their personal disposable incomes, which may be with the intention of acquiring some specific item, for example a car, or merely out of habit.
- Corporate savings consist largely of the retained profits of firms.
- Private savings consist of personal savings plus corporate savings.
- Government savings occur when the government gathers more in tax revenue than it spends, and is in a sense 'forced saving'.
- A large proportion of saving is contractual in that it consists of payments to insurance companies for life assurance or payments into pension funds.

It is unlikely that the rate of interest has any more than a marginal effect on any of these saving motives.

6 Savings behaviour

Experience of the 1960s and 1970s suggest that the growth of income is a significant influence upon savings behaviour. In 1969 the savings ratio (the ratio of personal savings to personal disposable income) was 8.1, this rose to 15.4 in 1980, before declining again as the rate of growth of incomes declined. By 1988 the savings ratio had declined to 5.

The reasons for the high level of the savings ratio in the 1970s and its decline in the 1980s are difficult to isolate. It is more convenient to consider the two periods separately.

- In the 1970s it is suggested that inflation was a major influence with the peaks in inflation and savings coinciding. One reason for this correlation is that inflation eroded the real purchasing power of the individual's liquid assets, and the level of savings was then increased in order to restore wealth to its previous level.
- The decline in the savings ratio, particularly in the latter half of the 1980s, is thought to be a consequence of the increased availability of credit and the more aggressive marketing of credit by financial institutions. A further influence may also be that the rise in property values increased the wealth of individuals to such an extent that they felt less need for savings and therefore increased their consumption. The reduction in the savings ratio together with the increased availability of credit were important elements in the UK consumer 'boom' of the late 1980s.
- The savings ratio rose from 5% in 1988 to around 11% in 1992. This increase may be attributed to a number of factors. One factor is the increased fear of unemployment, another is the high level of indebtedness incurred by consumers in the late 1980s, and also the reduction in wealth suffered by home owners due to the fall in property prices and the attempt by them to restore their net wealth to the previous levels. The increase in savings is a reflection of the lack of consumer confidence in the economy. The continued fear of unemployment and the failure of the property market to return to the boom of the early 1980s has continued to keep savings at a high level, despite low rates of interest, in the mid 1990s.
- Savings have been encouraged with the conversion of many building societies to banks and the incentives that have been on offer.

Self assessment questions

1 How is the demand curve for capital derived?

2 What is meant by the 'time preference' of individuals and what is its relationship to the supply of loanable funds?

3 Describe the function of the rate of interest.

4 Outline the 'classical theory' of interest rate determination.

5 Discuss the factors which determine the level of savings.

24
Profits

1 Factor reward

Profit is the reward to the entrepreneur. This factor payment is the return to the entrepreneur for
- Co-ordinating and setting to work the factors of production.
- Taking the risk of losing capital.

2 Risk

Risk is always present in capitalist production as production has to take place in advance of sale and it can never be known with certainty that the goods will actually be sold. Profit is therefore the reward for uncertainty bearing and differs from interest in the degree of risk involved; interest is associated with investments which are virtually risk free.

3 Concepts of profit

At this stage it is useful to recall the different concepts of profit;

- Normal profit (Chapter 14).
- Super normal profit (Chapter 14).
- Monopoly profit (Chapter 15).
- The difference between profits and the other forms of factor income is that it is a **residual** which is paid after the other factors of production have been paid out, and may therefore be **negative**. Also because factor costs and sales cannot be controlled or forecast profit tends to **fluctuate** more than the other factor incomes.

4 Functions of profit

The functions of profit in a free market economy are as follows:

- To ensure a supply of individuals willing to accept the risks of uncertainty.
- Super normal profits indicate to entrepreneurs which industries should expand and which should contract. Therefore super normal profits reflect consumers' preferences

for a good, and encourages the increased output of those goods which are in demand by consumers.

- Profits provide the resources necessary for expansion, both by re-investment in the firm, and by enabling the firm to offer higher rewards to the factors of production and attract them away from declining industries.
- Profits overcome the technical problems of how goods are to be produced by ensuring that production is carried on by only the most efficient firms. In a competitive industry the firms making the largest profits are those with the lowest costs, if other firms are to survive they will be forced to adopt the same methods of production, otherwise their prices will be too high and they will not be able to compete. Eventually they will make losses and go out of business, or leave the industry.

5 Profit measures

For most firms the most practical measure of whether they are making adequate profit is the rate of return on capital. The rate of return on capital is calculated as

$$\textbf{Rate of return on capital} \quad = \frac{\textbf{net profit}}{\textbf{fixed capital}} \times \textbf{100}$$

If this figure is too low then the firm would have to question either its profitability and how it could be improved or in extreme cases whether its capital could be invested more effectively elsewhere. Industrial investment which inevitably carries a degree of risk should for example, be making a better return than the capital would make on deposit with the bank where there is zero risk.

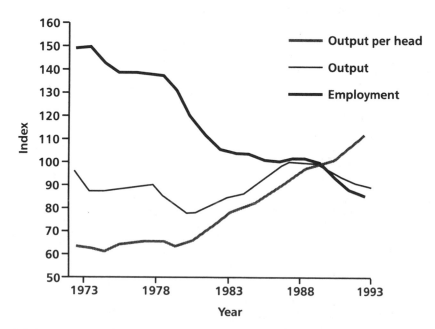

Figure 24.1

6 Profit in industry

The profitability of industry is a useful guide to the economic performance of a nation as this is an indication of how effective resource allocation has been in the past and to the potential of the economy for the future growth. Most countries experienced declining rates of return on capital since the mid 1960s, whilst the rate of return in the UK remained below that of its main competitors over the whole of the period. Following 1982 the UK experienced some recovery in profitability due particularly to the contribution of North Sea oil related industries and to a rise in the productivity of manufacturing industry which reduced costs.

The rise in manufacturing productivity which contributed to this improvement in profitability during the 1980s was greater in the UK than any other major industrialised country.

The recession of the early 1990s lead to decline in manufacturing output but output per head, productivity, continued to increase. The increase in productivity continued despite a fall in employment and a general contraction of demand for manufactured goods worldwide.

Self assessment questions

1 Distinguish between normal profit, super normal profit and monopoly profit.

2 In what sense is profit a residual?

3 What does the entrepreneur do in return for profit?

4 How does profit differ from interest?

5 What are the functions of profit?

6 What is meant by the statement 'profit is a residual of uncertain size'?

Consumer behaviour

1 Consumer satisfaction

Consumers will allocate their incomes between their chosen 'basket of goods' in a manner which maximises the útility (satisfaction) they receive from their expenditures.

Consumers compare the utilities they receive from various quantities of the goods they are considering buying to their prices. They will achieve the maximum satisfaction when the ratio of marginal utility to price between each good is equal, i.e.

$$\frac{\text{Marginal utility good 1}}{\text{Price of good 1}} = \frac{\text{Marginal utility good 2}}{\text{Price of good 2}} = \frac{\text{Marginal utility good 3}}{\text{Price of good 3}} \quad \ldots\ldots \quad \frac{\text{Marginal utility good N}}{\text{Price of good N}}$$

which can be alternatively represented as:

$$\frac{\text{MU good 1}}{P1} = \frac{\text{MU good 2}}{P2} = \frac{\text{MU good 3}}{P3} \quad \ldots\ldots \quad \frac{\text{MUn}}{Pn}$$

It can be intuitively reasoned that if a consumer could gain more utility by transferring expenditure from one good to another he would do so until the point where no further utility could be gained by re-arranging expenditures. At this point the MU to price ratios have been equalised.

2 Indifference curve analysis

In order to analyse the conditions for the consumer to be in equilibrium when faced with a given income and different relative prices we can utilise **indifference curve** analysis.

Indifference curves represent different combinations of goods available to a consumer, each combination yielding equal satisfaction to the consumer. As each combination of goods yields equal satisfaction the consumer is said to be indifferent regarding which actual combination is choosen. Table 25.1 represents different combinations of two goods A and B which will yield equal utility to the consumer. There would of course be many other possible combinations but here we have shown only four out of all those possible. As each of the combinations yield equal satisfaction the consumer will be indifferent as to which is actually choosen.

TABLE 25.1		
	Good A	**Good B**
1	35	5
2	20	10
3	10	15
4	5	35

These combinations are represented graphically in Figure 25.1. In Figure 25.1 the indifference curve I represents the four combinations of A and B shown in Table 25.1. Each point on the curve would be equally desirable to the consumer who would be indifferent to any combination available along the curve. The shape of the curve is convex when viewed from the origin, reflecting the 'law of substitution'. As one of the goods becomes scarcer as we move along the curve, the greater becomes its relative substitution value, and its marginal utility rises relative to that of the good which has become more plentiful; and the good which is becoming relatively scarcer requires larger quantities of the other good in return. The lines L–M represent the exchange terms at that point on the curve, i.e. 3:1. This is the **marginal rate of substitution** of A for B, which will maintain a constant level of utility along the curve.

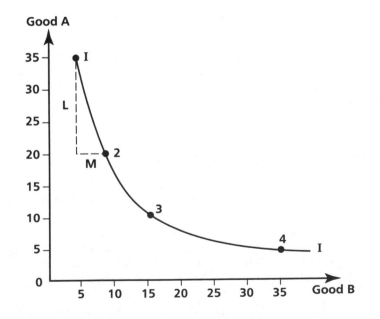

Figure 25.1

3 Indifference map

The indifference curve in Figure 25.1 is however drawn for a single level of income only, and as the consumers move to higher levels of income they will move to higher levels of satisfaction, and therefore a higher indifference curve. Figure 25.2 represents the **indifference map**, each indifference curve being relevant to a different level of income. The consumer will be indifferent between different combinations along any single curve, but as income increases can move to a higher curve. There is an infinite number of these curves, one for each possible level of income.

4 Consumer preferences

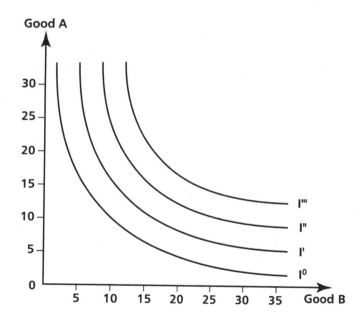

Figure 25.2

The indifference map refers only to **consumers preferences** if we are to establish which bundle of goods will actually be preferred, we need also to consider the relative prices of the two goods, and the consumer's income. If we assume that:

- consumer's income is £40
- the price of good A is £1 each
- the price of good B is £2 each

we can estimate the various quantities of each good which are available to the consumer given the income constraint and the prices of the two goods.

Table 25.2 illustrates some of the possible combinations of A and B. Clearly if 40 of good A are purchased there will be no income left for expenditure on good B, and vice versa if 20 units of B are purchased. Between these two extremes various combinations are available.

TABLE 25.2	
Good A	Good B
40	0
30	5
20	10
10	15
0	20

5 The budget line

From the data in section 4 we can derive the consumer's **budget line**. This is illustrated in Figure 25.3 by the line D–F and represents all the possible combinations of the two goods which can be purchased assuming the entire income is spent on the two goods. The slope of line D–F is the ratio of the price of good A to good B. It is important to note at this stage that the budget line represents what is **available to the consumers not their preferences.**

6 Consumer equilibrium

In order to establish which combination will be preferred, or **consumer equilibrium**, it is necessary to combine the consumer's indifference map with the budget line. The £40 budget line from Figure 25.3 is combined with the indifference map from Figure 25.2. The point of consumer's equilibrium is at E in Figure 25.4 with 20 units of good A and 10 units of good B. The consumer is in equilibrium where the highest attainable indifference curve is just tangential to the budget constraint. The consumer cannot move to a higher indifference

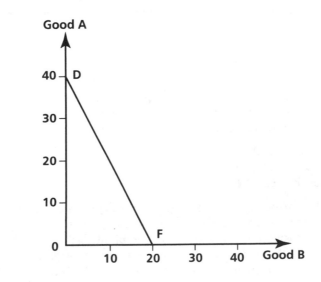

Figure 25.3

curve on current income, and will not move to a lower one as he will not be maximising his utility. At point E the consumer's marginal rate of substitution (MRS) of A for B is exactly equal to the ratio of the price of A to the price of B, from which it is evident that the condition for consumer equilibrium is

$$MRS_{AB} = \frac{P_A}{P_B}$$

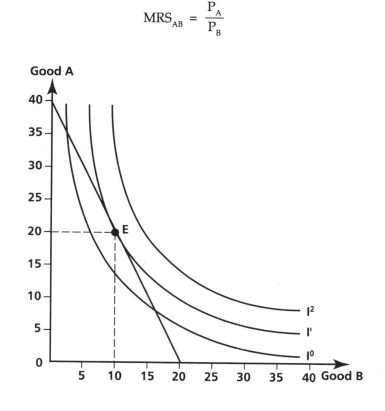

Figure 25.4

7 Changes of income

A reduction in income, or an equal rise in the price of both goods - which amounts to the same thing, will result in a shift of the budget line inwards towards the origin; the shift is parallel because the relative prices of the two goods are unchanged. In Figure 25.5 this is shown by the shift of the budget line D–F to NM.

Assuming both goods are normal goods, there will be a new equilibrium at E′ where the new budget line is tangential to the highest attainable indifference curve I′, with fewer of both goods purchased.

8 Income and substitution effects

An increase in the price of one good will shift the budget line in towards the origin. In Figure 25.6 the price of good B rises and the budget line shifts from DF to DM, the slope of the line changes because the relative prices of the two goods have changed. This leaves the consumer on the lower indifference curve I′ with a new equilibrium at E′. As one good becomes cheaper relative to another, and provided both are normal goods, then more of the good which has become cheaper will be purchased in place of that which has become relatively more expensive. This is referred to as the **substitution effect**, and in the diagram it can be seen that at E' more of good A is purchased than previously. Any price change also has an effect on **real income**, in this example the price increase reduces real

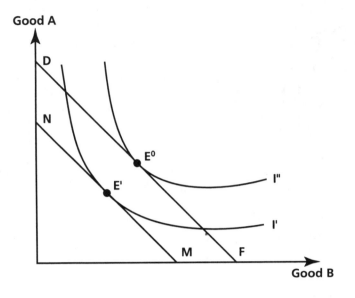

Figure 25.5

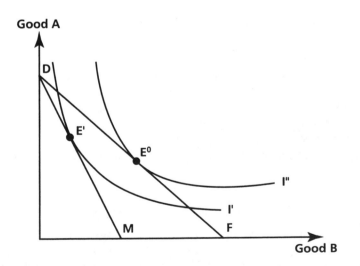

Figure 25.6

income and means that fewer of all goods can be purchased (and vice versa for a price reduction), this is referred to as the **income effect** of a price change. The substitution effect is represented by a movement along the indifference curve whilst the income effect is represented by a shift to another indifference curve. All price changes consist of both an income effect and a substitution effect and for all normal goods the income effect reinforces the substitution effect. However, for those inferior goods referred to as **Giffin goods** (see Chapter 4) a negative income effect may outweigh the substitution effect, in which case an increase in price may result in more of the good being purchased, and for a price reduction less being purchased. This provides a theoretical explanation for the regression in the demand curve for such goods, outlined in Chapter 4.

Figure 25.7 illustrates the method by which the income and substitution effects can be separated. The consumer is originally in equilibrium at E purchasing x of good B. The price of good B now rises and the budget line shifts in towards the origin to DG with the consumer now now in equilibrium at E' consuming x' of good B and more of good A which is now relatively cheaper. If now we keep the relative prices at their new level but alternatively give back to the consumer the amount of income by which the original price increase had reduced real income, we obtain the hypothetical budget line LM, parallel to the DG line because it faces the same relative prices but with the lower real income, we obtain equilibrium at E" with x" of good B consumed. The move from E to E" can only be as a consequence of the substitution effect. The movement from E to E' therefore represents the income effect. In the case of a Giffin good the new equilibrium position E" would lie to the right of E with more of good B consumed.

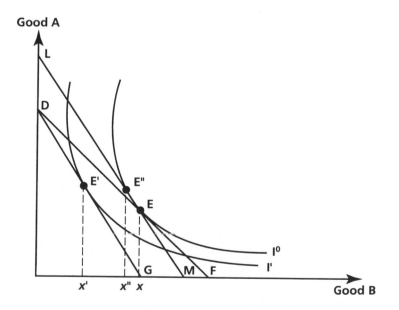

Figure 25.7

9 Income consumption curve

As household income changes, parallel shifts in the budget line occur and for each level of income there will be an equilibrium point at which each budget line is at a tangent to an indifference curve. This is illustrated in Figure 25.8 where successive increases in income are represented by the three parallel budget lines. In this example both goods A and B are **normal goods,** and by joining the equilibrium points for each level of income, the **income consumption curve (ICC)** is obtained. The income consumption curve shows how household consumption responds to changes in income with the money prices of the goods constant.

Figure 25.9 illustrates the ICC curve where good A is an inferior good and its rate of increase in consumption is very low relative to good B as income increases. Figure 25.10 illustrates the ICC for a **Giffin good**, where good A is so inferior that consumption declines as income rises.

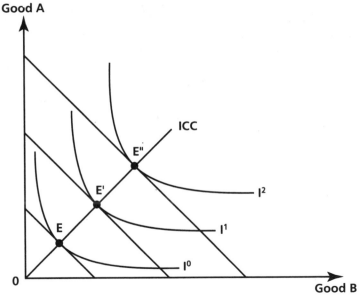

Figure 25.8

10 Price consumption curve

Changes in the relative prices of the two goods alter the slope of the budget line, as illustrated in paragraph 7. As the slope of the budget line changes, there will be successive points of tangency with the relevant indifference curves. Joining these successive equilibrium points as the **price of one good increases** produces the **price consumption curve (PCC)**. The price consumption curve shows how household consumption responds to changes in the price of one good with the price of other goods and income constant. This is illustrated in Figure 25.11 where the price of good A is constant while the price of good B falls through three stages, P, P^1 and P^2. This analysis underlines the theory of demand discussed earlier, which stated that with incomes and the price of all other goods held constant, then a reduction in the price of a good will result in more of it being consumed. The PCC in Figure 25.11 conforms exactly to that prediction and provides an alternative derivation of the demand curve.

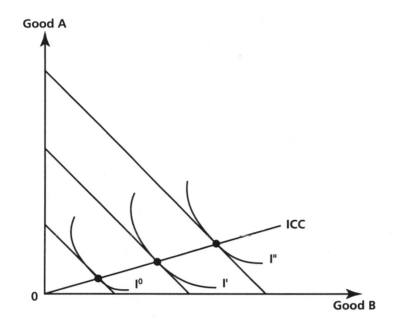

Figure 25.9

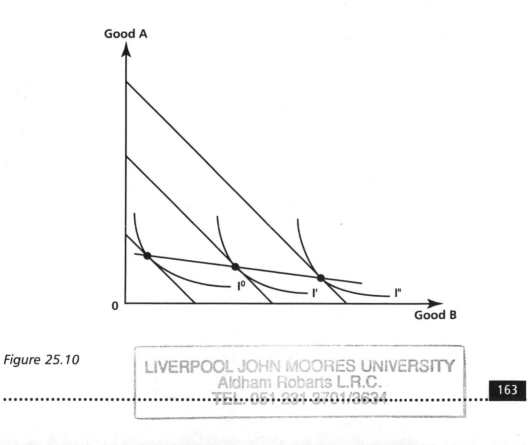

Figure 25.10

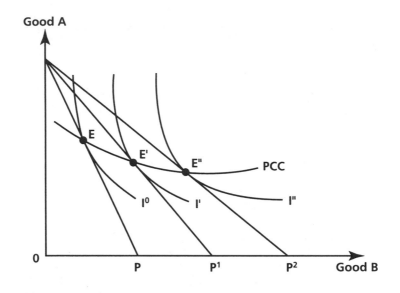

Figure 25.11

11 The demand curve

The alternative derivation of the demand curve by utilising indifference curves can be illustrated diagramatically using a similar analysis to that in 10 and Figure 25.11 above. Again we have the two goods A and B, the price of good A being held constant, while the price of good B is allowed to fall relative to it. This is illustrated in the upper segment of Figure 25.12 where the price of good B falls producing the three equilibrium points E, E′ and E″ with more of good B consumed as its price falls relative to good A. In the lower segment of the diagram the quantity demanded of good B is related to its price. Each of the equilibrium points in the upper segment produces one unique point on the lower segment where the price of the good is related to quantity. By joining the corresponding intersections, A, B and C, we can derive the downward sloping demand curve for good B. (This analysis ignores the income effect and more advanced study should allow for this by producing an income compensated demand curve).

Self assessment questions

1 What condition is necessary for a consumer to receive the maximum utility from expenditure?

2 Outline the method of construction and the significance of indifference curves.

3 What is meant by the consumer's budget line?

4 Using indifference curve analysis illustrate the conditions necessary for a consumer to be in equilibrium.

5 Illustrate how consumers' equilibrium is affected by:

   (i) A fall in the price of one good

   (ii) An increase in income.

6 Distinguish between the income and substitution effects of a price change.

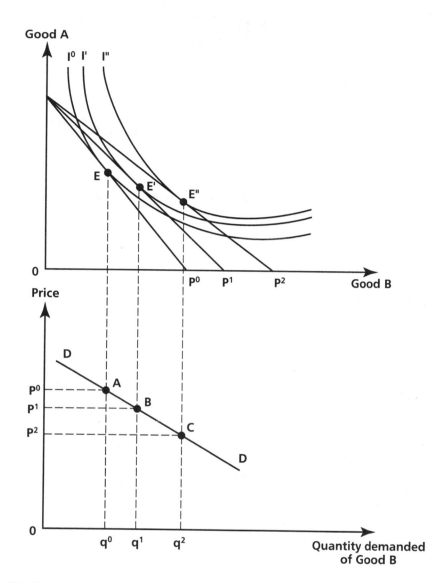

Figure 25.12

7 Illustrate the reaction of household consumption on two normal goods to a series of increases in income.

8 Illustrate diagramatically the distinction between the income and substitution effects in the case of a Giffin good.

Alternative theories
of the firm

1 Profit motive

The theories of the firm discussed so far are all based on the assumption that firms will always be motivated purely by the desire to maximise their short-run profits. In many firms today however, there is a clear division between the ownership and control of the organisation. Ownership is spread amongst shareholders whilst control over day to day decision making is in the hands of paid managers, and although some of the senior management, such as directors, may also have a minority shareholding, the majority of shares are held by individuals who have little or no contact with the firm on a regular basis and may only wish to exert influence through their votes at the annual general meeting of shareholders – if they are sufficiently interested to bother voting.

2 Alternative motives

The division between ownership and control of the organisation allows for the possibility that **managers may pursue some alternative objective than profit maximisation.** The alternative theories of the firm fall into two categories:

- Those which assume that managers attempt to **maximise some objective other than profits**, referred to as managerial theories of the firm.
- Those which allow for the possibility that **managers do not attempt to maximise any variable** but are motivated by some **alternative objective**, referred to as **behavioural theories** of the firm.

3 Baumol model

Baumol[1] proposed a model of the firm based upon the principle that the primary objective of the managers of a firm is to maximise sales revenue. Managers may seek to maximise sales revenue for a variety of reasons but mainly because the status and salaries of managers are generally linked to the growth of sales, as their performance is frequently judged by the growth of sales rather than profitability. In this model the need to make profits is still recognised but they act as a constraint on managerial behaviour rather than as an objective. It is recognised that there is a minimum level of profit which is necessary to meet the expectations of shareholders hence sales can be maximised subject to the constraint of earning the minimum level of profit. Sales maximisation does not refer to the maximisation of sales volume but the maximisation of sales revenue.

4 Sales maximisation

The Sales Maximisation model is illustrated in Figure 26.1 In the diagram profit is maximised at output Q^1 where the difference between total cost and total revenue is greatest, coinciding with the profit maximising rule of MC = MR (see Chapter 14, Appendix 2). The line Pc represents the firm's profit constraint which is the minimum level of profit necessary to satisfy shareholders. The sales maximising firm will therefore increase output beyond Q^2 up to the point where rising costs reduce profits to the level of the profit constraint which is output Q^2 in the diagram. The model therefore predicts that the **output of the sales maximising firm will be greater than that assumed under the profit maximising rule**. The only way in which the two outputs could coincide would be if the profit constraint was set at the point of profit maximisation.

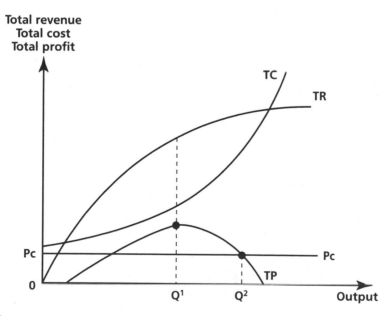

Figure 26.1

5 Objectives and the advertising budget

The Baumol model also suggests a **relationship between the firm's advertising budget and its choice of objectives.** This relationship is illustrated in Figure 26.2. In the diagram the shape of the total revenue curve assumes that the physical volume of sales can always be increased by advertising but eventually diminishing returns set in. It is also assumed that total revenue will vary in exactly the same way so any increase in physical sales volume resulting from increased advertising expenditure must always be accompanied by a proportionate increase in total revenue. The firm's other costs are assumed to be a function of advertising outlay and are added to advertising costs to obtain the total cost curve CC. The total profits curve TP is derived by subtracting total cost from sales revenue at each level of advertising expenditure. The line Pc is the profit constraint as described earlier.

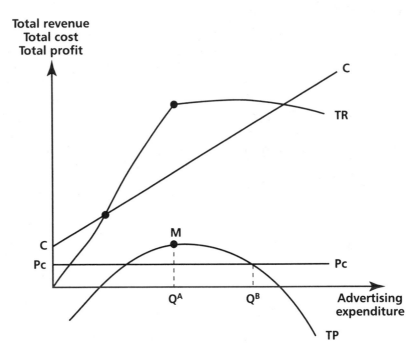

Figure 26.2

The advertising budget for the profit maximising firm is Q^A where total profit is maximised at M; however the constrained sales maximising firm will increase the advertising budget to the point where total profit just meets the profit constraint (Pc), i.e. advertising budget Q^B. The constrained sales revenue maximising firm will therefore advertise more than the profit maximising firm, because advertising will increase the sales volume and hence sales revenue, and advertising expenditure will increase to the point where the firm comes into conflict with the profit constraint.

6 Williamson model

O. Williamson[2] developed a **managerial utility model of the firm** based upon **managerial discretion** within large corporations. The model is based upon the assumption that shareholders do not exert direct control over the management of the firm and that the firm is not operating in a highly competitive market. Given these assumptions **managers pursue their own goals, subject to their being able to maintain control of the firm**. The goals of the firm therefore reflect the goals of the individual managers. The goals of the firm's managers are expressed in a managerial utility function which consists of three broad groups of expenditure:

- **Managerial salaries.**
- **Discretionary investment spending** on, for example, lavish offices and furniture.
- **Expenditures on the number of staff** reporting to a particular manager.

The greater the profits of the firm the more managers have the ability to undertake these forms of expenditure; hence **profits are important in the model.** However, the ability to undertake such expenditure also depends upon the ability of management to divert profits from shareholders. This is not a problem, however, as shareholders do not involve themselves in the management of the firm, and consist of a fragmented group which can be kept largely in ignorance of the detailed finances of the firm by the senior managements; which implies that **managers will enjoy a considerable degree of freedom regarding expenditures which enables them to maximise their own goals.**

7 Marris model

Marris[3] developed a model which emphasised **corporate growth as the main objective.** The model, as the others discussed so far in this chapter, assumes a separation between management and ownership (shareholders) and a sales market with a low level of competitive activity. It is also assumed in this model that **managers relate their salaries and status to the size of the firm;** any growth in the size of the firm therefore enhances their salaries and status within the firm. They therefore see the **growth of the firm as one of their major objectives.** On the other hand they fear takeovers by other firms as this may result in a loss of status and scope for salary increases. Takeover attempts are deemed to result from a depressed share valuation below the market valuation as judged by the firm considering the takeover. The main source of growth, through internal growth and diversification, depends upon a high level of retained profits for re-investment, however this creates a dilemma because a high level of retention implies a low level of dividend payments to shareholders which reduces the market valuation of the company. The management is therefore faced with a 'trade-off' situation between the dividend policy and retained profits and must seek the optimal balance between the two. The valuation ratio of a company is expressed as:

$$\text{Valuation ratio} = \frac{\text{Share price valuation}}{\text{Accounting valuation (book value)}}$$

and when the valuation ratio falls too low the firm becomes liable to takeover attempts. **The objective of the management can therefore be said to be to maintain the minimum valuation ratio consistent with deterring takeover attempts in order to maximise growth whilst retaining security.** Shareholders would prefer the maximisation of the valuation ratio through a higher dividend policy, management however will prefer a higher growth rate.

8 Managerial theories

The models discussed so far are generally referred to as **managerial theories** of the firm. These models stress the maximisation of some managerial objective although usually it is subject to some constraint. To the extent that they attempt to maximise an objective they have this feature in common with the profit maximising models. Another set of theories of the firm referred to as **behavioural theories**, which are based on the work of **H.A. Simon**[4] recognise that management faced with the complexity of the data and its imperfect nature recognise the impossibility of making the optimal decisions required for maximising behaviour and instead attempt to **'satisfice'**. This means that a firm's management will attempt to set itself **minimal standards of achievement intended only to ensure the firm's survival and a level of profit which is acceptable to shareholders.** Satisficing behaviour is not necessarily static as it involves a learning process. If a firm easily achieves its given objective it will review its aspiration levels in the following period upwards; failure may result in the stabilisation or lowering of aspirations in the following period.

9 Cyert and March model

Cyert and March[5] built upon the work of Simon and developed a model in which the firm was viewed as a **coalition of different interest groups**, which includes managers, shareholders, employees, the government, and creditors. These interest groups form a **loose coalition** but each group within the coalition will have **differing goals which may conflict;** these goals will receive attention in sequence as the particular group finds itself in a position to promote its interests according to how important it is perceived to be in the coalition at a particular time. **The conflict between different interest groups is resolved by a process of continuous bargaining**. Where groups fail to have their goals satisfied they are compensated by **'side payments'** which may be in the form of higher salaries, a higher status in the management structure, or more of the trappings of status such as a larger office or more office furniture etc. Shareholders are seen as a passive group who are easily satisfied, whilst the 'active' management group requires more than just side payments, and this group has most influence on the organisation's objectives. Management does not attempt to maximise profits, or any other variable, but **attempts to achieve an acceptable level of performance for a number of operational goals.** These goals reflect the objectives of different groups in the coalition and frequently conflict. The conflict between groups is resolved by the bargaining process described above. The organisational goals can be briefly summarised as follows:

- **A production goal** – production should be relatively stable and should keep the plant fully employed.
- **An inventory goal** – stocks should be maintained at a level which avoids 'stockouts' but without tying up excessive amounts of working capital.
- **A sales goal** – in terms of both revenue and market share, should be increased.
- **A profit goal** – should be sufficient to finance investment for growth, dividends, and internal budgets.

The goals which are actually pursued will be a **compromise reflecting the way in which conflicts are resolved within the particular organisation.** Provided that goals are satisfactorily achieved within one period then the same goals may be pursued in the following period. This satisficing behaviour gives rise to the possibility of **organisational slack.** Organisational slack refers to the situation where the firm has **more resources available than are necessary to meet current goals**. This serves several functions, firstly more resources are available for making side payments in order to resolve unsettled conflict within the organisation, and secondly during unfavourable market conditions the firm can reduce the level of organisational slack in order to maintain satisfactory performance levels. **The presence of organisational slack enables the firm to remain stable and therefore viable.**

10 Some conclusions

Observation in the real world suggests that businessmen frequently have little knowledge of their marginal costs and are not therefore in a position to make the optimal price and output decisions necessary for profit maximising theories. The managerial and behavioural theories attempt to overcome these weaknesses by making a different set of assumptions about the ways in which firms actually behave, and the prediction of these models are frequently consistent with the actual behaviour observed within large companies.

Self assessment questions

1 Explain what is meant by satisficing behaviour.

2 Discuss the effect of sales maximisation with a profit constraint on the output of the firm.

3 Discuss growth as a corporate objective.

4 What are the means by which goals are established in the Cyert and March model?

References

1 *Baumol, W.J., Business Behaviour, Value and Growth, Macmillan, New York, 1959.*

2 *Williamson, O.E., The Economics of Discretionary Behaviour: Managerial Objectives in a Theory of the Firm Prentice-Hall, 1964.*

3 *Marris, R., The Economic Theory of Managerial Capitalism, Freepress, Glencoe, ILL, 1964.*

4 *Simon, H.A., Theories of Decision Making in Economics, American Economic Review, Vol. XLIX June 1959.*

5 *Cyert, R.M. and March, J.G., A Behavioural Theory of the Firm, Prentice-Hall. 1963.*

The price mechanism

1 The basic problems

It will be recalled that the basic problems facing society are those of **what** to produce, **how** to produce it, and **for whom** the goods are to be produced. In a free market economy these problems are solved automatically by the interplay of market forces. According to Adam Smith 'each individual following his own self interest unknowingly brings about the general good', and the problems of what, how, and for whom are solved by what Smith referred to as the 'invisible hand' of the price mechanism.

2 Consumer sovereignty

Consumer sovereignty is said to prevail in a market economy because production and therefore resource allocation is in accordance with the preferences of consumers as expressed in the market place. If consumers prefer a good they will purchase more of it, i.e. it receives more 'consumer votes', as demand increases the market price will rise, and these 'price signals' indicate to producers which goods should be produced in greater quantities.

3 Welfare equilibrium

As the demand for goods changes so too do their relative prices, which results in a reallocation of the factors of production. In Figure 27.1, assuming goods X and Y are close substitutes, and there is a change in consumers' preferences away from X and in favour of Y. The price of X falls to P' and the price of Y rises to P'. The increase in Y indicates to entrepreneurs that Y is more profitable to produce and a transfer of resources will take place through demand and supply on the factor market and more of Y will be produced. Output and resource allocation has been in accordance with the preferences of consumers as indicated by the 'price signals'. In order to establish whether the price mechanism is capable of achieving an **optimal welfare equilibrium** it is necessary to consider next the concepts of **consumer's and producer's surplus.**

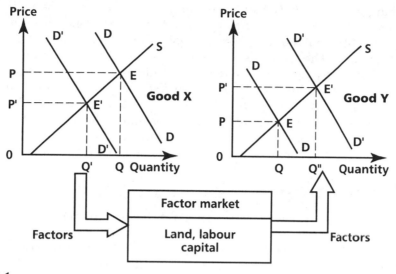

Figure 27.1

4 Consumer surplus

The concept of consumer's surplus refers to the **difference between the total utility from a given consumption level the consumer receives and the total expenditure at that consumption level.** This surplus arises because the consumer pays a uniform price on all the units purchased which is equal to the price of the last unit; however, we know from the

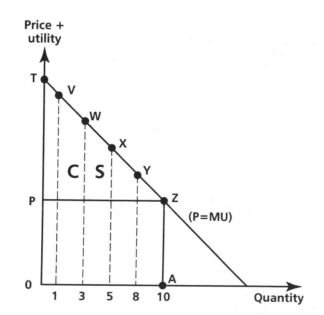

Figure 27.2

law of declining marginal utility that the earlier units are valued more highly than the last. Consumers will spend their budget on a good up to the point where **price = marginal utility (P = MU) only**; after this point they will purchase no more as they have maximised their utility. The concept is illustrated in Figure 27.2. The consumer pays price P for 10 units, however had only 1 unit been available the consumer would have paid price V, if 3 had been available price W, and so on. Only for the tenth unit is the P = MU, a surplus of marginal utility over price being gained by the consumer on all of the earlier units. The area of the triangle above P–Z is the **consumer's surplus**. At the tenth unit the consumer's evaluation of the marginal utility received from the additional unit is equal to the price, and total utility is area OTZA, but with expenditure only area OPZA.

5 Producer's surplus

Producer's surplus is the excess of market price over the minimum that would be necessary to persuade the producer to produce a given quantity. As the minimum return required to produce a given quantity is the marginal cost (MC), the **producer's surplus is the difference between market price and marginal cost.** As the marginal cost can be equated with the entrepreneur's opportunity cost then **producer's surplus is equivalent to the surplus over opportunity cost.** As the competitive firm's marginal cost curve is also its supply curve we can use the firm's supply curve to illustrate the point. In Figure 27.3 market price is P and quantity 10.

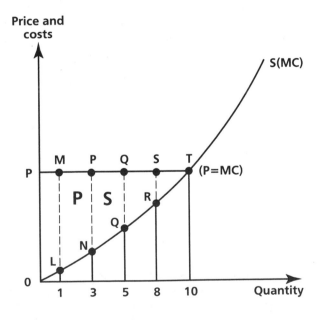

Figure 27.3

For the first unit however MC is L but price P is received, L–M is therefore the producer's surplus. For the third unit it is N–P, and so on. Only for the tenth unit is the market price exactly equal to the marginal cost, i.e. P = MC. The firm will not produce more than 10 because the MC would exceed the price received. Producer's surplus is therefore maximised at 10 units, and is represented by the triangle OPT.

6 Optimal output

If we assume a perfectly competitive industry it is possible to demonstrate that the competitive model can achieve optimal allocative efficiency. In Figure 27.4, the two previous diagrams are combined to illustrate a competitive market in equilibrium. We assume now that the demand and supply curves are market demand and supply curves. The market price $\bar{P}$ and quantity 10 maximises the total area of producer's and consumer's surplus. At this price each firm is operating at the lowest point on its average cost curve, **consumers are paying a price exactly equal to the marginal utility they receive from the last unit (P = MU) and producers are receiving exactly the marginal cost of producing that unit (P = MC).**

The situation is therefore optimal for society as a whole if all markets are in an identical situation. It is for the reasons outlined above that marginal cost pricing has been advocated as a rule for the nationalised industries to follow in their pricing policies.

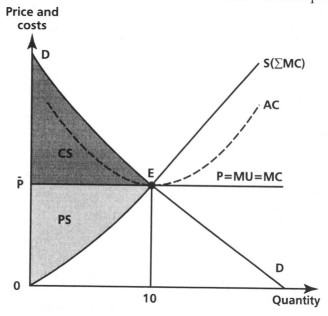

Figure 27.4

7 Consumer preference distortions

The concept of consumer sovereignty in the modern economy has been challenged by several writers, but in particular by J.K. Galbraith. Galbraith argues that consumer sovereignty is a myth and that the large corporations are in fact sovereign as they are able to create wants and impose them upon consumers by the use of advertising. Even if this overstates the case it is at least probable that advertising distorts consumers' preferences. Opponents of this view point to examples where consumers have resisted the attempts of large corporations to manipulate their preferences, in particular the failure of the Ford Motor Company to market their Edsel model in the 1950s.

8 Welfare economics

Given the existence of perfect competition in all markets it is theoretically possible for an allocation of resources to be achieved which is optimal for society as a whole. At the simplest level we can see that a competitive firm will produce at the lowest point on its average cost curve whilst the monopolist will not, also the competitive firm will produce a greater output at a lower price. It seems intuitively obvious therefore that competitive markets will be more beneficial to the consumer and anything which increases the competitiveness of markets will be to the benefit of the consumer. In order to reach this condition however we need a more objective criterion of what constitutes society's welfare, an area of study referred to as welfare economics.

9 Pareto optimality

In order to establish an objective criteria of social welfare, economists use the notion of **Pareto optimality**, named after the Italian economist Vilfredo Pareto (1848-1923) to whom the concept is attributed. A Pareto optimal allocation of resources is said to exist if it is not possible to reallocate resources so as to improve the well-being (or utility) of one person without making at least one person less well off (reduce their utility). To achieve a situation of Pareto optimality three conditions must exist within an economic system:

- **Allocative efficiency** – The economic system should ensure that the information regarding consumers' preferences are correctly conveyed to producers.
- **Technical efficiency** – The required output should be produced using the least possible resources or factors of production, i.e. the lowest unit cost method of production
- **Distributive efficiency** –The goods produced should be distributed precisely to those consumers desiring them.

10 Market failure

At this stage it may be worth reconsidering Figure 27.4. The conditions for Pareto optimality will exist when there is perfect competition in all markets. In the real world however, even if perfect competition could be established throughout the economy, there would still remain a number of conditions under which an economy would fail to achieve a situation of Pareto optimality. The situations in which perfect competition cannot achieve a situation of optimal efficiency are said to be situations in which **market failure** occurs. Three cases of market failure will be outlined here:

- **Natural monopoly**
- **Public goods**
- **Externalities**

11 Natural monopoly

This situation arises when the firm's long run average cost curve (LRAC) only reaches its lowest point at very large outputs, as illustrated in Figure 27.5. The firm has exploited all its economies of scale and is operating at its point of lowest cost at output Q^1. With such a cost structure the firm will be a natural monopolist because if faced with a competitor the firm can always exploit its cost advantage and temporarily lower its price in order to retain its dominance over the market. Natural monopolies tend to occur in industries where there are very high fixed costs which become less significant over high outputs, for example steel is impossible to produce viably on a small scale. Such industries are likely to be either regulated by government or taken into public ownership (nationalised) in order to control their monopoly profits. Such industries include steel, gas, electricity, and rail transport. It should also be noted that the marginal cost curve in Figure 27.5 lies below the long run average cost curve over most of its length, hence as long as market demand is consistent with output Q^1 the industry can operate the P=MC rule. However, if demand is below this level, for example DD, then the P=MC rule will produce a loss of A–B which will need to be subsidised from general taxation. Alternatively, the industry will be forced to set price = average cost (at C) and cover full accounting costs, which is not consistent with the P=MC rule for maximising society's welfare. (Note that output is also lower).

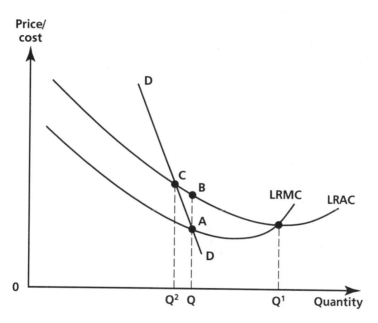

Figure 27.5

12 Public goods

Another class of goods which the price mechanism would fail to supply in adequate quantities are referred to as **pure public goods**. The essential characteristics of such goods are:

- They are **non-rival in consumption**, i.e. if one person consumes more, it does not mean that there is less for others as is the case with normal goods.
- They are in **joint supply**, i.e. if the supply is increased, it is increased to everyone.
- They are **non-excludable**, i.e. nobody can be prevented from consuming them.

The classical examples of such goods are: light from a lighthouse; law and order; and defence. The characteristics of such goods make it impossible to charge a user price. If rational consumers were asked to reveal their preferences for such goods and state how much they were prepared to pay for them, they would say zero because they would assume that they would receive all they wanted anyway. However, if each individual responded in the same way then there would be none provided, or at least there would be under provision, a problem referred to as the **'free-rider'** problem, which makes it impossible to make provision of such goods by a system of user prices. The only way such goods can be provided is collectively by governments through the tax system.

13 Externalities

Market prices fail to reflect **social costs** and **benefits**. Social costs may also be referred to as **externalities** or **spillovers**. Social costs occur when **actions by one party create costs which are borne by others**; or by society as a whole. For example, the act of production will involve private costs for the entrepreneur, but pollution in the form of smoke or effluent will impose costs upon the community at large. Conversely private expenditures, on for example health, education and housing may create social benefits not only to the individual but to society as a whole; for example, inoculations provide a private benefit to the individual but there is also the benefit to other individuals who will not now be at risk of catching the disease. **Market prices may therefore fail to reflect these external costs and benefits and will not bring about an optimal allocation of resources**.

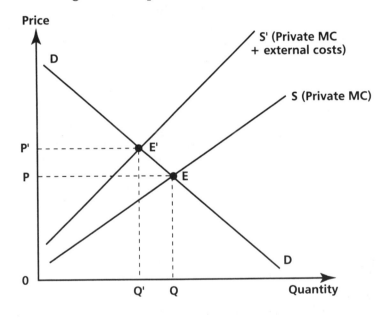

Figure 27.6

Externalities occur when a market has failed to emerge for a good because no-one is able to claim ownership of the good, hence there is a failure to allocate **property rights**, without which there can be no trading and therefore no price signals.

In Figure 27.6 when only private costs are taken into account, equilibrium price is P and quantity is Q, this does not however reflect the extra cost to society as a whole, or the marginal social cost. If social costs are included the supply curve, or marginal cost curve, becomes S¹ with the higher price P¹ and lower output Q¹. These external costs are unlikely to be incorporated in the decision-making of a private firm or individual as they will not be concerned with the effect of the marginal cost of their activities upon society as a whole, resulting in over-production of the good, i.e. Q instead of Q^1. The problem is therefore how to make individuals and firms incorporate social costs into their decision making or how to internalise them.

If, for example in the case of pollution of the environment by the emission of smoke from firms, a system of property rights could be established over the environment, and ownership given to the community, then bargaining could occur and firms would have to pay compensation if they wished to continue to pollute the atmosphere. In the absence of such an arrangement, firms will continue to pollute the atmosphere because it represents free disposal of waste, but by establishing property rights, a value is given to the resource of 'clean air' and a market begins to function, limiting the firms' use of it by putting a 'price' on its use.

Some commentators such as E.J. Mishan suggest the use of the tax system in the form of providing subsidies where there are external benefits, and taxes where there are costs, in order to bring about a level of output which is optimal for society as a whole. In Figure 27.7 market price is P and quantity Q. If there are external costs however the supply curve does not reflect the true marginal cost of production and the imposition of a tax raises the producer's costs to reflect both the private production costs and the external costs to society. As a consequence the price rises to P^1 and output falls to the optimal output for society, Q^1. Where there are external benefits private production costs do not reflect the benefits to society and the provision of a subsidy to the producer reduces costs, price falls to P^{11} and output increases to Q^{11}, with more of the socially desirable good produced. Provided the tax or subsidy is equal to the value of the externality the result should be optimal for society as a whole. In the diagram the tax would be A–B and the subsidy C–D in order to achieve the socially optimal outputs.

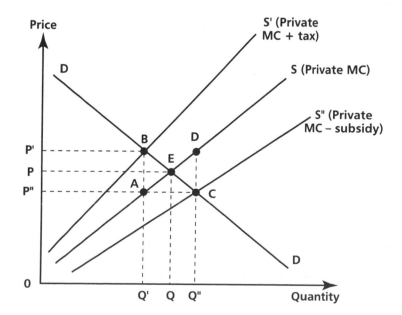

Figure 27.7

14 Merit goods

The market may fail to provide certain goods in sufficient quantities which society considers to be so essential that they should be provided free of charge. Such goods typically include education and medicine. Because such goods are considered to be so meritorious to society they are referred to as **'merit goods'**.

15 Asymmetric information

Information can be considered as a public good because once information is known to one person it is generally available to others; this makes it difficult to charge users a price sufficient to cover the costs of production, resulting in under production by the market.

Even where information is not a public good there may still be market failure. This arises in markets where there is a level of expertise present. The market failure occurs because in a transaction one party can take advantage of specialised knowledge in a way that affects the transaction itself. Such information is referred to as **asymmetric information**. The problem, generally referred to as the **principal agent** problem, can be illustrated by the example of taking your car to the garage. If you take your car to a garage and the mechanic diagnoses a certain problem of a serious and expensive nature you are unlikely to be in a position to make a valid assessment of the transaction, the same could be said of private medical provision. The classic example is the firm's managers who act as the shareholders principals but actually have more information than them, which enables them to pursue goals other than profit maximisation (see Chapter 26).

16 Pareto optimality – some conclusions

As mentioned in Chapter 1, criticism of the price mechanism on the basis of unequal income distribution is not valid, as the price mechanism and income distribution are separate issues. The definition of Pareto optimality has nothing to say about the **distribution** of economic activity.

In a modern economy it is unlikely that perfect competition could simultaneously exist in all markets and the conditions for the achievement of a situation of Pareto optimality cannot therefore be fulfilled. In reality there are imperfections in most markets, the majority of markets being either oligopolistic or monopolistic, as a consequence resource allocation in most markets will be less than perfect. This does not however mean that the competitive market has no relevance as it provides a useful yardstick for the measurement of the degree to which actual markets diverge from the competitive ideal.

Self assessment questions

1 What is meant by consumer sovereignty?

2 How does the market mechanism allocate society's resources?

3 What are the characteristics of 'pure public goods'?

4 Distinguish between private costs and social costs.

5 What is the 'free-rider' problem?

6 What are the market imperfections which prevent the price mechanism from achieving an optimal allocation of resources?

7 What are the conditions required for a situation of Pareto optimality to exist?

8 Outline three situations in which market failure may occur.

9 How could the tax system be utilised in order to internalise externalities?

10 Why are property rights important for the efficient functioning of a market?

Environmental economics

1 Green economics

Environmental economics, or '**green economics**' as it is popularly known, has become a major political issue during recent years. Theoretically environmental issues can be considered under the heading of **externalities** which have been dealt with in the previous chapter. The topic of environmental economics will be discussed here in a more general manner.

2 Property rights

The problems of environmental pollution as stated in the previous chapter arise from the fact that there are no **property rights** established over the environment and therefore a charge cannot be levied for its use. For firms, therefore, the environment offers the opportunity for the free disposal of waste, which reduces their production costs and increases their profits. As there are no property rights it is not in the interests of any single individual or firm to do anything to improve the environment as that individual would bear the cost but everybody would receive the benefit. The environment therefore has the same properties as a pure public good.

3 The 'tragedy of the commons'

David Hume writing in the 19th Century described the problem in an essay entitled 'The Tragedy of the Commons'. Common land was freely available to everybody in the community for the grazing of animals at no cost, and no single individual had the right to sell the land. As the land could be used without charge it would be overgrazed. If one person reduced their use of the land there was no guarantee that anybody else would, and hence there would be no incentive for any individual to desist. Neither would it be in the interest of any individual to improve the land, by installing drainage for example; as one individual would pay the costs but all would benefit; hence such improvements would not be made. As a consequence the land rapidly deteriorates and the un-regulated self interested behaviour of each individual produces a less-than-optimal solution for the group as a whole. Similar principles apply to the environment and its use by producers and consumers, and the problem is therefore one of how to internalise these costs into firms and consumers decision making, and how to regulate their behaviour in the interests of society as a whole.

4 Green issues

Much of the recent concern over 'green issues' has arisen in reaction to the mounting scientific evidence that serious damage is being done to the environment, to the extent that it may pose a serious threat to life on earth in the future.

5 Causes of concern

There appear to be several causes of concern for the environment including: **air pollution** through the emission of gases, disposal and shipment of toxic waste, excessive use of **pesticides** in agriculture, and pollution of the seas through the **dumping of industrial waste** and sewage. Also the **spillage of oil** in accidents involving tankers, which threatens marine life and coastlines and hence in turn endangers the tourist industry.

6 'Green wealth' and GDP

The source of these pollutants are the by-products of industrial production, and the waste products from consumption. It is not merely that they make the environment unpleasant but that they are also a danger to health and safety, and as such impose severe costs upon the community. These costs are not included in conventional measures of wealth such as Gross National Product (GNP). Often these problems become worse as nations enjoy rapid economic growth because as incomes rise so too do the social costs. Professor David Pearce of London University has suggested that in addition to the conventional measure of GDP there should also be an estimate of **'green wealth'**. Conventional GDP measures plus this estimate would provide an overall assessment of sustainable growth which can be achieved without damaging the welfare of future generations. Indonesia for example, which achieved annual GDP growth of 7% from 1971 to 1974, would be measured as having sustainable growth of only 4% because it had depleted its reserves of finite resources in achieving that growth.

7 Air pollution

It is air pollution which is causing the greatest concern. Air pollution arises from many sources, but the effects of it are impossible to contain as they 'spill over' national boundaries and create a world-wide danger. For example, in the construction of power stations on the east coast of England it has been possible to overcome the local dangers resulting from the production of sulphur oxides by building very high chimneys; unfortunately the sulphur dioxides produced by the burning of fossil fuels such as coal, falls on the

Scandinavian countries in the form of '**acid rain**' which destroys forests and poisons streams, killing the fish stocks. Again the costs of the externality are not borne by those creating them.

8 Motor vehicle emissions

The greatest concern has been expressed over air pollution. This concern has been expressed at both local and international level. At a local level exhaust emissions from motor vehicles and industrial emissions of various gases into the atmosphere affect the health of the community and make the environment generally less pleasant. The major pollutant arising from vehicle emissions is carbon monoxide, a highly toxic gas which poses a serious threat to health and safety of individuals. In cities during the rush hour in hot weather carbon monoxide concentrations can reach quite dangerous levels.

9 The 'greenhouse effect'

The greatest concern however has been expressed over the dangers of global warming arising from the emission of gases into the atmosphere. Global warming refers to increases in temperatures throughout the world as a consequence of the 'greenhouse effect' which itself results from gaseous emissions into the atmosphere. The most important of the 'greenhouse' gases is carbon dioxide (CO_2). The increase in the amount of CO_2 in the atmosphere is a consequence of both the increase in the burning of fossil fuels and also the increasing rate of deforestation, particularly the depletion of the world's rain forests in areas such as the Amazon Basin of Brazil. Forests have the effect of converting CO_2 into oxygen but deforestation reduces this process resulting in increased concentrations of CO_2. Deforestation occurs as trees are felled for timber or areas cleared for farming. The practice of clearing the rain forest by burning large areas actually worsens the situation by the emission of additional CO_2.

10 Global warming

The 'greenhouse effect' arises because the greenhouse gases, such as CO_2 form an insulating layer around the earth. The sun's rays can pass through this layer and heat the earth's surface but the heat is unable to escape, resulting in a rise in global temperatures. This rise in the earth's temperature is expected to be sufficient to cause severe disruption to the world's weather patterns and also lead to the melting of the polar ice-caps. These changes are expected to create floods, droughts, violent storms and changes to the distribution of the world's food production. Unfortunately it is predicted that the UK output alone of CO_2 will increase by 25% by the year 2005.

11 CFC's

The production of chlorofluorocarbons (CFC's) have been the cause of further widespread concern. CFC's have a wide range of uses but are best known for their use as propellants in aerosol containers, and in refrigerator cooling systems. Recent evidence has indicated that the release of CFC's into the atmosphere causes damage to the ozone layer. The destruction of the ozone layer in the earth's atmosphere increases the risk of skin cancers and also adds to the greenhouse effect. The EU has agreed to ban the use of CFC production by the year 2000. This, however, indicates the worldwide nature of the problem, because at the same time countries such as India and China see the refrigerator as a major and immediate public health requirement and the Indian government have set the objective of eventually having a refrigerator for every family.

12 Sources of global warming

The make up of global warming and the sources of carbon dioxide emissions are illustrated in Fig. 28.1.

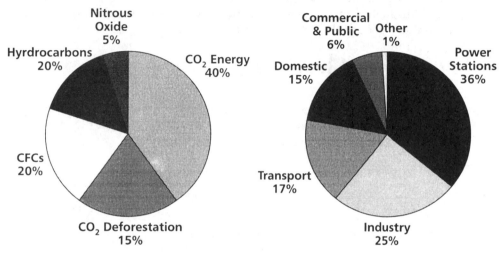

Figure 28.1
Sources: UK Atomic Energy Authority and CEGB from the Lloyds Bank Economic Bulletin

13 Pollution control

There are no immediate 'solutions' to these global dangers, however the threat is so great that action has to be taken. The discussion will now look at some of the proposals which have been made for the reduction or gradual elimination of the worst of the dangers. At this point it is worth re-reading the section on externalities and the theoretical analysis of how the tax system could be used to internalise them in Chapter 27.

14 Externalities

It will be recalled from Chapter 27 that E.J. Mishan suggested that where there is an external cost causing private and social costs to diverge then a tax should be imposed on the producer which is equivalent to the external costs imposed; in this instance damage to the environment. This tax results in an adjustment to price and output which reflects the costs to society as a whole, i.e.: the external cost is internalised – or taken into account. This approach is more popularly referred to as the **polluter pays principle.**

15 The polluter pays principle

The **polluter pays principle** operates by the imposition of taxes on goods which are damaging to the environment. This tax could be similar to **Value Added Tax** and would be the equivalent to the difference between **private** and **social costs.** Products such as CFC's which are known to damage the ozone layer would therefore cost extra, depending on how damaging they were considered to be. This would have the following effects:

- The industry has an incentive to find alternative, less damaging substitutes in order to avoid the tax and thereby reduce their costs.
- There would be investment in technology and equipment which reduce pollution, because this would now show a greater rate of return.
- The higher prices would encourage consumers to seek lower cost pollution-free alternatives, i.e. the higher prices as a consequence of the tax would reduce consumer demand on those goods which cause pollution.

16 Taxation and lead-free petrol

The reduction of the tax on lead-free petrol is an example of the use of the tax system to improve the environment. Taxation on lead-free petrol was reduced by 10p per gallon. Consequently the use of lead-free petrol increased from 1% to 24% of the market by the end of 1989. This is illustrated in Figure 28.2.

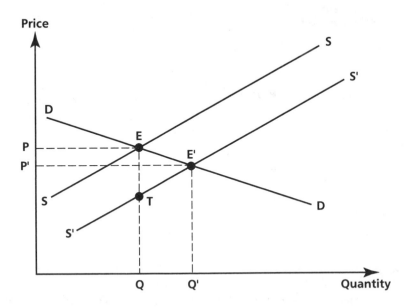

Figure 28.2

In Figure 28.2 demand curve DD represents the demand for lead-free petrol. At the original price, P, quantity Q is demanded. The tax reduction (E–T) is represented by a shift in supply from SS to S^IS^I with the greater quantity Q^I demanded at price P^1. (The elastic demand curve DD represents the fact that the price elasticity of demand between brands of petrol is higher than the price elasticity for petrol as a product).

17 Professor David Pearce

The UK government has voiced support for the polluter pays principle in its proposed legislation for the control of pollution, the proposals being based upon a report by Professor David Pearce, advisor to the Department of the Environment. Through the proposals it is intended that the consumer will pay for the pollution he creates by using the product. Furthermore there are plans for the labelling of environmentally 'friendly' products in order to give additional guidelines to consumers.

18 Mr. P. Foley

Mr. Patrick Foley, deputy Chief Economic Advisor to Lloyds Bank supported the polluter pays principle and he also suggested the labelling and taxing of goods according to the amount of environmental damage their production or consumption causes. In his report Mr. Foley said that pollution taxation would correct, rather than create, market distortion as the price of goods would then reflect their environmental cost and would encourage research into methods of reducing pollutants.

19. Pricing the environment

Another form of taxation suggested to the government, and under consideration by the National Rivers Authority, is to make manufacturers who cause pollution pay for it. Instead of the environment representing a free source of disposal for waste products manufacturers would be forced to pay a charge for its use. This would be in the form of a license, the cost of which would be proportionate to the amount of pollution caused. This would provide a strong incentive for polluters to find ways of reducing emissions of gases and discharges of effluent into the environment. This approach involves the estimation of a cash value for the environment, which may prove a difficult task given the inevitable differences in personal valuations.

20 Standards

An alternative to the use of the tax system in the control of pollution is the setting of **standards**. Legislation can be enacted, which sets standards and regulations over wide areas of activity. For example, since 1983 all new cars in the USA have been fitted with 'catalytic converters' which reduce the amount of harmful gases in car exhaust, the same rule applies to cars sold within the EU by the mid 1990s. Similar regulations could be imposed upon other industries over a wide range of activities. The problems with this approach are the technical and financial ones of monitoring and control. Such an approach is not new, however, and has worked in the past, an early example being the Alkali Acts of 1906.

21 Green policies

Concern over environmental issues resulted in a promise by the UK government to introduce a 'green bill' in an attempt to reduce levels of environmental pollution and to encourage the recycling of paper and other materials. The House of Commons Energy Select Committee called upon the UK government to take the lead in developing appropriate technologies for combating the greenhouse effect. It also proposed tax incentives to encourage business to economise on energy use, the linking of vehicle excise duty to fuel efficiency and a government campaign to highlight important issues. The 1994 Budget Speech mentioned specifically that:

> 'In some cases taxes actually do some good, by helping markets work better and by discouraging harmful or wasteful activities.'

The same budget also proposed a 'landfill' tax to be levied on waste disposal, with a rate of £7 per ton.

22 Some conclusions

It is difficult to see how market forces alone could bring about a solution to the world's environmental dangers. The problem when seen in a world setting seems almost insurmountable and exhortations to those in dire poverty to reduce their living standards still further for the benefit of future generations is unlikely to meet with success. For example, peasant farmers in Brazil who burn the rain forests to grow more food in order to feed their families, are understandably more concerned with today than the future. Furthermore, their governments, burdened by debt repayments to the west, can afford to do little to encourage them to desist. The dangers facing the human race appear to be so grave however that solutions must be found, and if economists can help in finding a solution it may be the greatest contribution that the science can make to human welfare.

Self-assessment questions

1 What is the relationship between environmental pollution and property rights?
2 What is meant by the 'greenhouse effect'?
3 Discuss the 'polluter pays' principle.
4 How can the tax system be used to reduce environmental pollution?

Glossary of economic terms

Accelerator Coefficient. The amount of additional capital required to produce a unit increase in output in the accelerator model.

Accelerator – Multiplier Model. A model which explains the fluctuations in the trade-cycle through the interaction of the accelerator principle and the multiplier.

Accelerator Principle (The). A capital stock adjustment process which proposes that the level of investment varies directly with the level of income (output).

Ad Valorem Tax. Indirect taxes which are a 'proportion of value'.

Advanced Countries. Industrially advanced countries with the highest levels of national income per head.

Aggregate Monetary Demand (AMD). The total demand for goods and services in the economy. Assumed to consist of the demand for consumption goods (C), plus investment goods (I) by firms, plus the demand by government (G), plus the demand for exports (X) minus imports (M). As aggregate demand determines the level of output (income) it also determines the level of employment. It is central to the Keynesian model of demand management. Therefore AMD = C+I+G+(X–M).

Aggregate Supply. The total supply of all goods and services available from domestic production plus imports to meet aggregate demand.

Arbitrage. The practice of buying in one market at a low price and reselling in another market at a higher price. Eventually the practice will eliminate the price difference between the two markets. May occur with the switching of short term funds between financial markets with different interest rates or exchange rates.

Asymmetric Information A cause of market failure where some economic agents have more knowledge or information than others. The parties do not have equal bargaining power. In the theory of the firm it is seen in the separation of ownership from control in that managers have more information than shareholders.

Autonomous Investment. That proportion of total investment not determined by economic factors, such as the rate of interest, but by factors such as technical innovation.

Average (Total) Cost. The total cost of production divided by output to give the average cost of production per unit.

Average Propensity to Consume (APC). The proportion of national or individual income which is used for consumption purposes.

Average Propensity to Save (APS). The proportion of national or individual income which is saved, i.e. not used for consumption. It is the complement of the APC and therefore measured as 1–APC.

Balance of Payments. An account summarising the UK's transactions with the rest of the world. Divided into two sections: the current account and the capital account. The current account is composed of visible trade (goods) and invisible trade (services). The capital account consists of flows of funds for investment purposes and loans. There may be a surplus or deficit on the current account.

Balanced Budget. Refers to the budget of the central government which is said to balance when the receipts from taxation are sufficient to meet the government's expenditure. Since 1945 UK budgets have generally been in deficit.

Balanced Budget Multiplier. The proposition that even when an increase in government expenditure is exactly matched by an increase in taxation it is still possible to have a multiplier effect on national income

Bank of England. The central bank of the UK. Established in 1694 and nationalised in 1946 and given independence in 1997. It is responsible for implementing the government's monetary policy and acting as banker to the government. It is also responsible for the issue of bank notes and coins through the issuing department.

Barriers to entry. Characteristics of a market, either economic or technical, designed to raise the costs of firms wishing to enter that market and so deter them from entering.

Beveridge Report. Prepared by Lord Beveridge in 1942 on social insurance and allied services at the request of the government. It contained a plan for social security based on three aspects; a health service, child allowances, and full employment.

Birth Rate (Crude). The average number of live births occurring in any year for every 1000 of the population.

Black Economy. That part of a country's economic activity which is not officially recorded as part of the national income. Referred to as 'black' as it is untaxed. Currently about 10% of gross domestic product in the UK.

Brandt Report. The report of the commission of inquiry into the problems of the developing countries under the chairmanship of Herr Willy Brandt. Published in 1980 entitled 'North-South: A Programme for Survival'.

Bretton Woods Conference. Bretton Woods, New Hampshire 1944, a conference to consider proposals for the settlement of post-war payments problems. Resulted in the system of fixed exchange rates, the IMF and the IBRD.

Budget Deficit. Occurs when the central government's expenditure exceeds revenue from taxation, the deficit covered by borrowing. Advocated by Keynes (J.M.) as part of the process of demand management. The normal situation in the UK in the post-war period.

Budget Surplus. When central government revenue exceeds expenditure. In the UK a surplus, established 1987, is referred to as public sector debt repayment (PSDR).

Built-In (Automatic) Stabilisers. Features in a modern tax and benefit system which tend to automatically dampen down fluctuations in income and employment. For example, as incomes rise recipients move into higher taxation brackets which dampens down inflationary tendencies. As unemployment rises the increase in welfare benefits automatically increases, maintaining the level of aggregate demand.

Capital. The stock of physical assets utilised in the act of production which are themselves the result of production. Generally taken in economics to be buildings, plant and machinery, i.e. physical goods or real capital.

Capital Expenditure. The purchase of fixed assets such as plant and equipment.

Capital Formation. Net (new) investment in fixed assets, i.e. additions to the stock of capital.

Cartel. A group of firms within an industry who collude to regulate prices and/or output in their own interests, thereby reducing or eliminating competition .

Central Bank. A feature of all developed economies, it is the instrument by which governments implement monetary policy and control banking and credit creation. In the UK also a bankers' bank and 'lender of last resort' to the discount market.

Clearing Banks. Banks which utilise the London bankers clearing house for the settlement of claims among themselves. Generally taken to be the same as the commercial banks.

Closed Economy. A simplifying device for purposes of national income analysis by which an economy is assumed to have no imports and no exports, i.e. no foreign trade.

Cobweb Theorem. A model in which the quantity currently supplied depends upon the price which prevailed in the previous market period. Usually applied to farm commodities, it explains the wide fluctuations in price and output which may occur in agricultural markets.

Common Agricultural Policy (CAP). The system of intervention in agricultural markets within the EC designed to maintain farm incomes and encourage output. 'Intervention prices' are maintained by the commission for each commodity by buying and storing surplus production.

Complementary Goods. Goods are complementary when a reduction in the price of one of the goods results in an increased demand for both goods, for example a reduction in the price of cars increases the demand for both cars and petrol.

Consumer Surplus. The surplus of utility which consumers receive resulting from the difference between the market price they actually pay for a good and what they would be prepared to pay rather than go without it.

Consumption Function. The relationship between aggregate consumption expenditure and aggregate disposable income in an economy. A central feature of the Keynesian model, in which consumption is assumed to be a function of income.

Consumption Goods. Goods purchased by consumers for final consumption rather than for the production of further goods. May be single use, e.g. ice-cream or durable, e.g. refrigerators.

Contestable Markets. Oligopolistic markets where the barriers to entry are low hence the threat of potential entry modifies the behaviour of the firms in that market. A perfectly contestable market is one without sunk cost, making entry easier.

Corporation Tax. A tax on the profits of companies.

Cost-push Inflation. Inflation which arises from increased cost factors such as the price of materials or labour. It is independent of the level of demand.

Currency Appreciation. An increase in the exchange rate of one currency relative to others in a regime of flexible exchange rates. In a fixed exchange rate system referred to as revaluation.

Currency Depreciation. A fall in the exchange rate of one currency relative to others in a regime of flexible exchange rates. In a fixed exchange rate system referred to as devaluation.

Cyclical Unemployment. Unemployment which results from the downward fluctuations in the trade cycle.

Death Rate (Crude). The number of deaths occurring in any year for every 1000 of the population.

Deflation. A reduction in the general level of prices brought about by monetary and fiscal policies designed to reduce the level of economic activity.

Demand. The desire and ability of consumers to purchase an amount of a particular good or service.

Demand Curve. A curve which relates the prices of a commodity to the quantity the consumer is willing to purchase. Conventionally price is shown on the Y axis and quantity on the X axis. The demand curve slopes downward from left to right reflecting the 'law of downward sloping demand '.

Demand-pull Inflation. Inflation which results from aggregate demand in the economy exceeding the full employment output of goods and services. If aggregate demand exceeds aggregate supply prices will rise, if these price rises are sustained the result is inflation.

Demand Shift. An increase or decrease in the quantity demanded at each price as a consequence of a change in factors other than price e.g. taste, preferences, incomes. Represented by a shift in the entire demand curve upwards to the right in the case of an increase, and downwards to the left in the case of a decrease.

Depression. A severe downturn in the trade cycle characterised by high levels of unemployment, in particular the UK 1929 - 1933.

Developing Country. A country with a low level of GNP per head, which has not reached the stage of industrialisation.

Development Areas. Those areas in the UK which because of their high levels of unemployment are deemed by the government as qualifying for special assistance e.g. development grants.

Discount Market. Also referred to as the money market, consists of the banks, discount houses, and accepting houses. The market deals in Treasury bills, bills of exchange, and short dated bonds. It is important to the authorities for its role as an intermediary between the Bank of England and the banking system.

Diseconomy. The long-run tendency for average cost of production to rise after reaching a minimum point. Generally due to problems of administration and co-ordination.

Disposable Income. Personal income, after the deduction of taxation and receipt of benefits, available for spending or saving.

Division of Labour. The breaking down of a task into its simplest components in order to facilitate specialisation of labour and/or mechanisation. The basis of surplus production and the exchange economy.

Dumping. The sale of excess production at the marginal cost of production in export markets in order to increase profits in the domestic market or to eliminate competition.

Durable Goods (Consumer). Consumer goods such as refrigerators which are not consumed immediately but over a period of time. More accurately it is the service or utility which they yield which is consumed.

Economic Growth. Refers to growth of national income which is generally taken to imply rising living standards.

Economic Rent. The return to a factor in fixed supply which is considered to be a surplus the size of which is determined by the price of the factor. Where there are transfer earnings it is the surplus payments over the transfer earrings.

Economies of Scale. As the scale of production increases with successive increases in plant size there is a tendency for average costs per unit of output to decline due to the economies of large scale production.

Elasticity of Demand (Price). The degree of responsiveness of quantity demanded to changes in price. In response to a price change therefore total revenue may increase, stay unchanged or fall. Measured by the formula

$$PED = \frac{\text{percentage change in quantity demanded}}{\text{percentage change in price}}$$

The resulting coefficient of elasticity will be, < 1 (inelastic), = 1 (Unitary), or > 1 (Elastic).

Elasticity of Supply (Price). The degree of responsiveness of quantity supplied to changes in price. The coefficient of elasticity of supply is measured as:

$$PES = \frac{\text{percentage change in quantity supplied}}{\text{percentage change in price}}$$

Entrepreneur. The name given to an individual in economics who manages and owns his own business, thereby providing the capital and enterprise, accepting all the risks, and receiving all the profit as a reward.

Equilibrium. An important concept in economics referring to a situation where opposing forces are in balance and there is no further tendency to change. In a market equilibrium would exist when the quantities demanded by consumers was exactly equal to the quantity supplied by producers at the prevailing price.

European Monetary System (EMS). An attempt by the EU to establish a system which would keep the fluctuations between the currencies of the member countries within narrow bands.

European Union (EU). Established by the Treaty of Rome in 1957 for the purposes of creating a customs union. The objective of the treaty was to eliminate obstacles to the free movement of goods, labour and capital between the member countries; to establish an external tariff, and a common agricultural policy (CAP). The basic idea is to form a large trading bloc to compete with other large blocs such as the USA and USSR. The original 6 member countries had grown to 13 by 1987.

Exchange Rate. The price of a currency expressed in terms of another currency, which is also the rate at which the currencies can be exchanged.

Excise Duties. Taxes levied upon goods for domestic consumption.

Externalities. An externality exists when the production or consumption of a good by one party imposes costs or benefits upon another party, but will not be included in the decisions of the party creating them.

Factors of Production. The essential requirements necessary for production to occur, namely, land, labour, and capital. These are combined by enterprise to produce economic goods.

Fiduciary Issue. Paper money not backed by gold. The fiduciary issue is backed only by confidence in the currency unit. The note issue is now entirely fiduciary.

Fixed costs. Those costs of production which in the short run do not change with output, e.g. rent, rates, interest.

Fixed Exchange Rates. A system whereby a group of trading nations agrees to maintain a par value for their own currency relative to the others through intervention on the foreign exchange markets. Such a system was operated by the IMF members from 1947 to 1973.

Flexible Exchange Rates. A system whereby the rate of exchange is determined by the market forces of supply and demand.

Frictional Unemployment. Unemployment which results from the time lag between labour becoming unemployed and locating a suitable vacancy. It may exist therefore during periods of high employment and can be a consequence of job changing.

Friedman, Milton. Professor of Economics at Chicago University and a leading exponent of monetarism.

Full Employment. In terms of gross domestic product it is a measure of the output which the economy is capable of when all its resources are employed. For labour it is taken to mean that everyone who desires a job at the current wage rate is employed and only frictional unemployment remains.

Funding Operations. The process of changing the structure of the national debt by converting short term debt to long term debt.

General Agreement on Tariffs and Trade (GATT). Established in 1948 with the objective of reducing tariffs and other barriers to trade, and to encourage free-trade between the 88 members. Replaced by the World Trade Organisation in 1995.

Gilt-edged Securities. British government securities with fixed rates of interest, traded on the Stock Exchange.

Gold and Foreign Exchange Reserves. Stock of gold and foreign currency held by a nation for the settlement of international indebtedness if required to do so.

Gross Domestic Product (GDP). The total output of goods and services produced by the economy over a year, expressed as a monetary value.

Gross National Product (GNP). Gross domestic product plus income earned from overseas investment owned by UK residents less income paid abroad to foreign residents.

Horizontal Integration. The merging of different firms at the same stage in the manufacturing process.

Import Duties. Taxes imposed on imported goods. May be ad valorem (according to value) or specific (per unit).

Import Quotas. A form of import control whereby only certain quantities of specified goods may be imported.

Imports. The goods and services which enter a country from overseas sources for domestic consumption.

Income Tax. A tax on incomes. In the UK deducted by employers at source and paid to the Inland Revenue; referred to as Pay-as-You-Earn income tax (PAYE).

Incremental Capital-Output Ratio (ICOR). The ratio of net investment to the change in output over a given period, i.e. the additional output gained from new investment.

Inflation. A generalised and sustained rise in the price level or a fall in the value of money.

Inflationary Gap. The excess of aggregate monetary demand over aggregate supply measured at the full employment level of national income.

Interest. The reward for foregoing current consumption.

Interest, Rate of. The price of borrowed money. The price a borrower must pay a lender to compensate for foregone consumption.

International Bank for Reconstruction and Development (IBRD). Known also as the 'World Bank'. Established at the Bretton Woods Conference 1944 with the purpose of encouraging capital investment for the reconstruction and development of its member countries either by making loans from its own funds or by the direction of private funds to suitable projects.

International Monetary Fund (IMF). Established at the Bretton Woods Conference 1944 and effective from 1947. The purpose of the fund was to encourage international co-operation on trade and payments. Was responsible for the management of the fixed exchange rate system which operated from 1947 to 1973, and provided a fund to assist member nations with temporary balance of payments difficulties.

Investment. Expenditure on capital goods.

J-Curve. Name given to the observation that following a currency depreciation the balance of payments generally deteriorates before eventually improving. If graphed the trend looks like a letter J.

Keynes, John Maynard (1883-1946). Author of *'The General Theory of Employment, Interest, and Money'* (1936). His writings formed the basis of the post-war economic policies of demand management, i.e. The 'Keynesian Model' in which governments utilise their own expenditure in order to manage the level of demand.

Kondratieff Cycle. After the economist M.D. Kondratieff, the proposal that there are long term cycles in the trade cycle with peaks and troughs every 50-60 years.

Laffer Curve. After Professor Arthur Laffer, a curve relating tax revenue to the tax rate.

Lean Production. The removal of all non value adding activities from manufacturing process from the suppliers to the final customer. The focus of operation is on core, or value adding, activities. Includes the elimination of waste through rigorous control of quality and inventory.

Lender of Last Resort. An essential feature of the role of a central bank is the provision of a facility for loans to the banking system when required to do so, in the UK through the medium of the discount market. This lending is done on the central bank's own terms which enable it to influence the general level of interest rates and the money supply.

Liquidity. The ease with which an asset can be converted into money.

Liquidity Preference. The extent to which individuals desire to hold their wealth in the form of money rather than other assets such as bonds.

Long-run. The period of time in which the firm can adjust all its factors of production, both variable and fixed.

Macroeconomics. The study of the aggregate performance of the whole of gross national product and the price level.

Marginal Cost. The additional cost resulting from a small (or single unit) increase in the output of a good.

Marginal Product. The increase in total output resulting from a small increase in one factor of production whilst all the other factors are held constant. Can be applied to labour, land, or capital i.e. marginal productivity of labour etc.

Marginal Propensity to Consume (MPC). The proportion of each additional unit of income which is devoted to consumption. As not all income is normally consumed the value of the MPC is usually less than one. The size of the MPC determines the slope of the consumption function and plays an important part in the multiplier process.

Marginal Propensity to Save (MPS). The proportion of each additional unit of income which is devoted to saving. As income is either consumed or saved it has a value of 1 - MPC.

Marginal Revenue. The change in a firm's total revenue which results from the sale of one additional unit of output.

Marginal Utility. The increase in total utility gained by increasing the quantity consumed of a good by one unit.

Marginal Utility, Law of Diminishing. As successive units of a good are consumed the extra utility received from each additional unit tends to diminish. Underlies the theory of demand.

Microeconomics. The study of individual economic units, consumers and firms and the ways in which they make their decisions. The central concept is the role of the market.

Minimum Lending Rate (MLR). The rate of interest at which the central bank is prepared to lend to the banking system in its role as 'lender of the last resort'.

Monetarism. The school of macroeconomic thought that suggests that the money supply is the most important factor in determining the level of expenditure and prices.

Money. Anything which is generally accepted in exchange for goods, or in settlement of a debt.

Money Supply. The quantity of money which exists in an economy at any single time. As there is no single definition of money different definitions may be utilised for operational purposes such as M0, M4 etc.

Monopoly. A market in which a single seller controls the entire output of a good or service.

Multiplier (The). A measure of the effect on national income of a change in one of the components of aggregate demand. A central element in the Keynesian model of demand management, generally referred to in terms of investment or government expenditure.

Calculated as:–

$$\frac{1}{1 - MPC}$$

where MPC = marginal propensity to consume.

National Debt. The cumulative total of outstanding debts owed by successive governments

National Income. The aggregate or total income of the nation which results from economic activity, measured in monetary terms, over a specified time period - usually a year.

Net Investment. Gross expenditure on capital formation less investment to replace worn out plant and equipment

Oligopoly. A market which is dominated by a few large sellers i.e. there is a high degree of concentration in the market.

Open Market Operations. The purchase and sale of securities by the central bank on the open market in order to influence the stock of financial assets and thereby indirectly the lending of the banks.

Opportunity Cost. Cost defined in terms of the value of the alternatives which have been foregone in order to achieve a particular objective.

Optimum. The best outcome which can be achieved from a given set of variables.

Organisation of Economic Co-operation and Development (OECD). Established in 1961, the organisation's aims are the encouragement of economic growth and high employment among the member countries, to assist in the economic development of the less advanced member and non member countries, and the expansion of multilateral world trade. The organisation functions through a number of committees and publishes a regular statistical bulletin.

Organisation Of Petroleum Exporting Countries (OPEC). A group of fourteen countries who are the major producers and exporters of crude oil. Established in 1960, it attempts to fix prices and production quotas for crude oil exports.

Participation Rate. The proportion of the population who are of working age and are part of the labour force.

Per capita income. Income per head of population. i.e.

$$\frac{NY}{population}$$

Phillips Curve. The empirical proposition put forward by Professor A.W. Phillips in 1958 that there was a significant inverse relationship between the level of unemployment and the rate of change of money wages.

Precautionary Motive. Money held for the purpose of meeting unforeseen expenditures.

Principal-Agent Problem. A feature of asymmetric information resulting in the problem of resource allocation which arises from the difficulty of imposing contracts forcing agents to act in their principals best interests.

Prices and Incomes Policy. Government policy aimed at regulating the rate of increase of wages and prices in order to control inflation.

Privatisation. The sale of government holdings in nationalised industries to the private sector.

Productivity. The rate at which output flows from the use of factors of production. Often used in terms of productivity to mean efficiency.

Public Sector Borrowing Requirement (PSBR). The deficit between the income and expenditure of the public sector, in particular central and local government. Usually financed by debt sales to the 'non bank' private sector, borrowing from the banking system, borrowing from overseas, or by issuing more cash to the public.

Quantity Theory of Money. A theory of the relationship between the supply of money in an economy and the price level.

Rate of Return. Net profit as a percentage of capital employed in a business. An important measure of business efficiency.

Real Income. Income measured in terms of the goods and services it will actually purchase.

Real Wages. Money wages deflated by an index such as the retail price index to give the actual purchasing power implied.

Reflation. Policy measures designed to raise the level of aggregate demand closer to the full employment level of national income.

Rent–see Economic Rent

Retail Price Index. An index used to express current retail prices in terms of a base year. The index is based on a weighted average of typical consumer expenditure patterns.

Saving. Desisting from using income for current consumption, as income which is not consumed must be saved. Note that this is not investment, it only becomes investment when the saved funds are used to acquire an asset.

Seasonal Unemployment. Unemployment which arises from the seasonal nature of some types of work such as the holiday related industries.

Short-Run. The time period during which the firm can adjust only its variable factors of production, such as labour.

Social Cost. Occur when actions by one party create costs which are borne by others or by society as a whole.

Special Deposits. Cash deposits by the clearing banks with the Bank of England in response to a directive by the Bank in order to restrict credit creation.

Special Drawing Rights (SDRs). Used by the IMF to finance international trade. Countries with balance of payments difficulties could draw up to 125% of the quota they contributed to the fund, but with increasingly severe conditions regarding their domestic economic policies imposed upon them.

Speculative Motive. Money balances held for the purposes of avoiding losses on a declining securities market. An innovation to monetary theory by J.M. Keynes to explain liquidity preference.

Structural Unemployment. Arises out of fundamental changes in the industrial base of the economy. Generally associated with the decline of 'staple' industries concentrated in the regions, hence also related to the 'regional problem'.

Supply. The quantity of goods or services which a producer is willing to put on to the market at the prevailing price during a particular time period.

Supply Curve. A curve illustrating the relationship between the market price of a good and the quantity supplied. The convention is that price is shown on the Y axis and quantity on the X axis. Supply curves generally slope upwards to the right.

Supply-Side Economies. A view of macroeconomics which emerged during the 1970s but with much in common with the classical tradition of economics. Supply-side economists take the view that output is determined by real variables and therefore stress the importance of the growth of the supply of the factors of production and technological change. They also suggest that fiscal and monetary policy cannot influence real output in the long run.

Tariff–see Import duties

Terms of Trade. The ratio of the index of export prices to the index of import prices. If export prices rise more quickly than import prices the index rises and represents an improvement in the terms of trade and vice versa.

Trade Barrier. A term used to describe any restriction on international trade imposed by government.

Transactions Demand for Money. The demand for cash balances to finance normal expenditures between receipts of income.

Transfer Earnings. The returns to a factor of production which are just sufficient to keep it in its current use. Any excess over transfer earnings is economic rent.

Transfer payments. Income transfers between different groups in society. For example from the employed to the unemployed, or students in the form of grants. Deliberately excluded from national income calculations as to include them would result in 'double counting'.

Treasury Bills. One of the means by which the government covers its short term borrowing requirement. The bills have a maturity of 91 days after which they are redeemable with interest. The amounts vary between £5000 and £1 million and are issued by tender to the money market.

Unemployment, Natural Rate of. The unemployment which remains when the labour market is in equilibrium. Such unemployment is therefore considered voluntary in the sense that the unemployed labour is not willing to work for a sufficiently low wage. Associated with the monetarist view.

Utility. The satisfaction derived from the consumption of a good or service.

Value Judgement. A statement of opinion which cannot be validated by appeal to the facts.

Vertical Integration. The merging of firms at different stages of the production process, either backwards towards the source of raw materials or forwards towards the retail stage.

World Trade Organisation. Established to monitor world trade and encourage free trade. Set up in 1995 to replace GATT.

Yield. The income from a security as a percentage of its current market price.

Index